THE
SENSITIVITY
CODE

Books by Theresa Cheung

Dream Dictionary A to Z
21 Rituals to Change Your Life
The Premonition Code
21 Rituals to Ignite Your Intuition
Answers from Heaven
An Angel Called My Name
The Ten Secrets of Heaven
The Afterlife Is Real
The Moon Fix
The Birthday Encyclopedia

THERESA CHEUNG

THE SENSITIVITY CODE

Thread

Published by Thread in 2020

An imprint of Storyfire Ltd.
Carmelite House
50 Victoria Embankment
London EC4Y 0DZ

www.thread-books.com

ISBN: 978-1-83888-514-4
eBook ISBN: 978-1-83888-513-7

The information contained in this book is not advice and the
method may not be suitable for everyone to follow. This book is not
intended to replace the services of trained professionals or to be a
substitute for medical advice. You are advised to consult a doctor on
any matters relating to your health, and in particular on any matters
that may require diagnosis or medical attention.

Water is fluid, soft, and yielding. But water will wear away rock, which is rigid and cannot yield. As a rule, whatever is fluid, soft, and yielding will overcome whatever is rigid and hard. This is another paradox: what is soft is strong.

– Lao Tzu

CONTENTS

A NOTE

In 2020 the world found itself plunged into an era of social distancing and self-isolation due to the coronavirus. People with sensitive personality traits may be uniquely equipped to deal with these challenges given their contemplative nature and the empathy and intuition that defines them. Indeed, they have much to teach and offer during these uncertain times when the world has never needed to be reminded more of the importance of empathy and kindness.

PREFACE

A Brief Note for Everyone

Some people are born sensitive with a rich inner life. They live their lives vividly through the lens of emotion and with their senses perpetually on high alert. Others are less highly sensitive. But to be human is to have the potential for greater sensitivity within us, because research suggests that gentle traits, such as empathy and intuition, are hardwired into our DNA. Even the toughest among us, whom others might label 'insensitive', will experience times in their lives when their innate sensitivity is activated and they feel overwhelmed, or sense and feel things they can't explain.

Although this book speaks directly to the estimated 20 percent of the population researchers and psychologists identify as exhibiting highly sensitive traits, it is important to point out from the outset that it is not written exclusively for them. It is for everyone, because everyone can feel delicate from time to time, with sensitivity triggered by certain situations or experiences. In a world that increasingly seems to value extroversion, competitiveness and zero empathy above all else, we need to learn more effective ways to understand and harness the secret strength and power of gentleness that lies within us all.

So, while *The Sensitivity Code* is a vital resource for the highly sensitive, the advice offered here is for everyone who has ever gone through sensitive times or simply longed for the world to be a little kinder.

INTRODUCTION

Highly Sensitive Times

Since you are reading this book, the chances are that you have always felt life deeply or are feeling rather sensitive right now.

Perhaps you've been told you are *over*sensitive, or that you should stop taking everything so seriously. The need to be alone on a regular basis to explore your rich inner world, or escape a constant stream of irrelevant stimuli, may be a strong force within you. Seeing acts of unjustified cruelty, particularly towards animals, feels like a knife in your heart. You simply can't observe violence on screen as others seem to do. You feel it. Your empathy towards the vulnerable and the underdog is a cross you have to bear. Crowds, bright lights, strong scents, loud noises and unexpected changes in routine can unsettle you greatly. Or perhaps you feel you have to hide your true feelings and pretend to be someone you are not, or that you are an outsider or imposter who doesn't belong.

Or do you feel that in a tough, 'survival-of-the-fittest' world – where the way to get noticed is to shout the loudest – your mild-mannered, heartfelt approach just doesn't cut it? That your desire to empathise with another person's viewpoint, rather than ignore or challenge it, and to be gentle rather than aggressive means you haven't got what it takes to thrive?

If any of the above sounds familiar, you are indeed a sensitive soul and this is the perfect book for you. *The Sensitivity Code* offers proven skills and techniques that can help you better understand your sensitive traits and learn why harnessing rather than repressing them is essential for a meaningful and fulfilling life. What you read and learn here will certainly help you 'toughen up', but *not* because you are someone who needs 'fixing'. Quite the contrary. You'll discover that sensitive individuals can't change their nature and should never need to; feeling sensitive is nothing to be ashamed of. Feeling things deeply and being on high alert to what is going on around you – both what can and can't be seen – is an essential genetic trait that might even have the power to save humanity from itself.

I truly believe that gentle souls are needed now more than ever. I believe this because I have dedicated my life to empowering sensitive, open-hearted people by collating their true stories in my books and seeking to understand and champion their traits. I believe this because I would describe myself as a sensitive soul and there have been so many highly sensitive times in my own life. Let me share with you a very recent one, which was, in fact, the catalyst for this book.

How I got here

It was one of those surreal 'how on earth did I get here?' moments.

In November 2018 I found myself sitting opposite controversial comedian and Hollywood star Russell Brand. We were recording episode 71 of his iconic *Under the Skin* podcast in his studio. If you get a chance to view it on YouTube, you can both see and hear me talking about being a highly sensitive person in an insensitive world. At several points in the interview I am close to tears, particularly when I talk about unintentionally viewing images of animal cruelty on my newsfeed and being so traumatised that I was unable to go online for months afterwards.

During the interview my heightened nerves are brutally exposed. People often say they can me read like a book. My thoughts and feelings are written all over my face, as is often the case for people who are sensitive by nature. I look and sound like a rabbit caught in the headlights. That's exactly how I felt: overwhelmed. I don't blame Russell for being a little impatient at times during the interview, as he likely expected a guest who was 'cool' and 'together' and not so clearly out of their comfort zone.

You may wonder why on earth I put myself through such an ordeal, given that my natural preference is to be an invisible author hiding behind my computer and writing about feelings rather than talking about them. The reason I went on the podcast was because I have grown increasingly alarmed in recent years by the marginalisation of sensitive traits, like empathy, kindness, compassion, imagination and intuition.

The invisible but healing and transformative power of these gentle traits is what I promote in all my spiritual books. As a bestselling author I felt it was high time for me to endorse this message more publicly. The problem was that I had never done something quite so high profile before, or with someone quite so famous. I'd thrown myself into the deep end and I was drowning. Sitting in the studio, I felt there was too much to absorb. My heart was beating so hard I thought it would break; my senses were split into a thousand different pieces. Instead of listening carefully to Russell's voice so I could answer his questions eloquently, I only heard the sound of his pen tapping on the desk and the hum of the microphone. Instead of looking at Russell, I was distracted by the movements of the people in his production team, who were outside the studio looking in, and, for some reason, by the pile of ripe grapes sitting between us on the table. When Russell reached out to eat a few of those grapes my focus was entirely on how many he would eat!

Despite being in sensory overload, I struggled through the interview somehow. When it was over, Russell and his production team were kind and professional, but I felt I had made a terrible mistake – I had let myself, and them, down. I felt great empathy for them, as they had clearly wanted an academic and insightful debate and what they had got instead were the dreamy babblings of an incoherent 'snowflake'. As I stifled my tears and shook Russell's hand afterwards, he said with a broad and warm smile that my interview had 'tripped him out'. Coming from someone with Russell's dramatic backstory of recovery from addiction and drug use that was not easy to hear!

I had sincerely hoped my interview would raise awareness of the value of gentle traits, such as intuition and empathy, and a mystic approach to life with an audience unfamiliar with my writing. However, I didn't think I got my point across effectively at all. I felt like I had done more damage than good to the cause, perhaps even set it back, because it was clear to me that I would very likely be ridiculed. Social media can be an extremely harsh and intolerant place. I convinced myself that the episode was such a disaster it would never actually be broadcast. I sent Russell a card profusely thanking him and his team for giving me their time. I wanted to reassure them that I was absolutely fine, even though I wasn't. For the next four months I relived and reanalysed that interview over and over again in my mind. Each time it felt even more excruciating. I also suffered from stomach pains and headaches for weeks afterwards, as whenever I'm overly stressed and anxious it always impacts me physically.

In March 2019 I was finally getting over the ordeal and feeling mighty relieved that, since nearly five months had passed, the interview would probably not air, when it suddenly *did* air. I dived for cover and was physically sick when a friend told me they had seen the trailer online.

Then something remarkable happened. Contrary to the ridicule or 'crybaby' comments I had fully been expecting, to my surprise I received far more messages of support than condemnation. Many said they wanted to know more about what I was saying and commented on how honest I had been to try to even argue the case for a more emotional and intuitive approach to life. Some of Russell's fans even said they wished he had given me a chance to talk more about being sensitive amid a material world. Others wrote to me to say they identified fully as they, too, were highly empathetic, intuitive and inclined towards the mystical. They asked me where they could find out more about how to manage their sensitivity in an insensitive world.

The relief was incredible but it was also a huge wake-up call. I really should have known better. Even though I was fully aware of my tendency towards being oversensitive, when placed in a high-stress situation with a supremely confident celebrity, I regressed. I fell right back into the sensitivity trap of excessive worry, overanalysis and fear of offending, disappointing or being criticised by others. And, once again, all that self-inflicted stress had been completely unnecessary. It was time for me to stop apologising or feeling ashamed of who I was and to see my sensitivity as a strength.

Reading and feeling such unexpected support from people unfamiliar with my mystic writing was one of the most empowering moments in my life. It became crystal clear to me that the world might just be ready and willing, perhaps even eager, to hear more about the power of being sensitive. The positive reaction to wearing my heart on my sleeve – and from an online audience that doesn't suffer fools gladly – convinced me that people who are sensitive need to boldly step out of their own shadows.

Spreading the word

I sincerely want this book to help gentle people recognise their own true worth and feel empowered and at peace, rather than fragile and conflicted and ashamed of feeling things deeply. I would like this book to offer gentle people coping tools to help them manage their emotions and navigate insensitive environments. I would also like this book to help sensitive people identify the red flags of toxic relationships. It is a truth universally acknowledged that sensitives typically attract self-serving narcissists and energy vampires into their lives, and in some cases, it can take their forgiving hearts a long time to wake up to the damaging emotional abuse. Last, but by no means least, I also want this book to eliminate damaging misconceptions about being sensitive.

Setting the sensitivity record straight

Here are the most common and frustrating misconceptions about sensitivity or being sensitive, followed by some facts that challenge them:

- *Sensitive people are shy and introverted.* There are sensitive extroverts, too – about 30 percent of sensitives are extroverts.
- *Sensitives are fragile, ineffective 'snowflakes'.* Many defining characteristics of sensitive people, such as their empathy, passion and creativity, make them exceptional business leaders or influencers on the world stage, for example, Walt Disney, Jacinda Arden, John Lennon and Princess Diana to name but a few.
- *Sensitive people are pushovers who have no firm convictions of their own.* Empathy is a defining characteristic of sensitives, but it is not an endorsement of another person's viewpoint; rather it's simply respecting and listening to that viewpoint.
- *Sensitivity is a women's issue.* Up to 50 percent of sensitives are men.
- *Gay men are prone to being sensitive.* This is a social stereotype that equates being gay with being more feminine and, as stated above, sensitivity is not a feminine issue.

- *Highly sensitive people are prone to depression and anxiety.* There may be an increased risk of anxiety and depression but it is important to point out that depression is a serious medical condition that needs treatment and many factors contribute to the likelihood of depression, including past trauma, chemical imbalances and genetics. Lack of self-awareness, whether a person is highly sensitive or not, can also increase the risk.

- *There is a strong link between hypersensitivity and autism.* Those with autism may well have sensory issues, for example, finding things like bright lights or loud noises overwhelming, but this does not mean that everyone with sensory issues has autism. There are major differences between high sensitivity and autism, but chiefly autism comes with 'social deficits' (less response in brain areas associated with empathy) and high sensitivity does not[1].

- *Sensitive people are too weak and self-doubting to become effective leaders, stand up to narcissists or succeed in a harsh and critical world.* Not so. Once they are armed with self-awareness and the tools and techniques to turn their gentleness into a strength, sensitive people are an unbeatable force.

- *Sensitive people are empaths because they feel what others feel.* But not all empaths are sensitive, i.e. they soak up emotions but not all the other stimuli from an environment as sensitives tend to do.

- *Sensitive people need to 'toughen up'.* They can't, because being sensitive is who they are. They are born that way.

---

1 Acevdeo, B., *et al.* (2018) 'The functional highly sensitive brain: A review of the brain circuits underlying sensory processing sensitivity and seemingly related disorders.' *Philos Trans R Soc London B Biol Sci*, Apr 19, 373.
It is worth noting that people with ADHD may be more likely to have hypersensitivity.
https://www.additudemag.com/hypersensitivity-disorder-with-adhd

I used to buy into all these negative associations – until I knew better. This book will dispel all this fake news, especially the notion that a sensitive person needs to 'toughen up'. They simply can't. It's like telling someone who is taller than average that they should be shorter. Just as being tall is not a flaw, being sensitive is not a flaw. It is not an illness or a choice people make, either. It is how they are born. According to experts,[2, 3] it is an innate trait with research[4, 5] indicating that at least three sets of genes may contribute to it. Some highly sensitive people may have all or some of these 'sensitive' genes and intriguingly all three impact the brain and nervous system in some way.

Sensitive people are born to be gentle and to experience life on high alert through the lens of their feelings and senses. They are not better or worse than anyone else, just different. Although they may have traits in common, they are not all the same. Every sensitive person is unique, just as every person who is taller than average is unique. Indeed, the fact that the genetic coding for sensitivity continues to survive natural selection suggests that for evolutionary reasons, for the survival of the human race, it is beneficial that some people can see, feel and sense things others cannot. It offers an evolutionary advantage and exists and will continue to exist because it is the one true force that drives humanity towards greater connection. Empathy, intuition, creativity, gentleness and compassion are personality traits that unite rather than divide, and they are all defining traits of the highly sensitive individual.

---

2 Dr Elaine Aron: https://hsperson.com/recent-genetic-findings

3 Licht, C. *et al.* 'Association between sensory processing sensitivity and the 5-HTTLPR short/short genotype.' Centre for Integrated molecular brain imaging.

4 Todd, R. *et al.* (2015) 'Neurogenetic variations in norepinephrine availability enhance perceptual vividness.' *Journal of Neuroscience*, 35(16).

5 Chen, C. *et al.* (2011) 'Contributions of dopamine-related genes and environmental factors to highly sensitive personality: A multi-step neuronal system-level approach.' *PLoS One*, 6(7), e21636.

In a nutshell, we are all born with a unique genetic code. The key to a fulfilling life is not to repress, deny or try to hide our uniqueness but to make the most of what life has given us. *The Sensitivity Code* will help you to understand that if you are born highly sensitive or suddenly find yourself feeling sensitive, this is not a weakness. Rather, it is a strength, and a healing gift both for yourself and for the human race.

Naturally sensitive

My passion is to show that our urge towards sensitivity is entirely normal and natural. It is part of who we are. We should not try to diagnose it; we should not consider it something out of the ordinary. We should simply understand it, embrace it and learn how to harness its healing power. That's why in this book you will find that I prefer to avoid labels and simply refer to people with sensitive traits as sensitive, gentle or mystic people, rather than highly sensitive people or HSPs, which is the term scientists and psychologists tend to use.

What's in this book

The Sensitivity Code is the book I wish I had been able to read decades ago to help me better navigate my way whenever life overwhelmed me. Like many people who are sensitive, I spent years feeling like a misfit or that there was something wrong with me. I wasted so much energy trying to 'fit in', giving far more than I received and constantly stifling my feelings or trying to be someone I was not, all in order to impress or not offend others. My self-esteem plummeted every time I felt anxious interacting with confident or aggressive people. If only I had understood my true nature and learned coping strategies not merely to survive but to *thrive* in an insensitive world.

The pages that follow present my own experiences, as well as true-life stories from other people who are sensitive, along with proven strategies to help people with sensitive traits flourish. There are seven chapters and you are encouraged to read them in order, as they will guide you on a journey of personal and spiritual growth.

Chapter 1 explains what sensitivity is, current scientific research into sensitivity and how to identify sensitive traits in yourself and others. Chapter 2 digs deeper and explores the psychological blind spots or challenges faced by delicate souls, as well as the advantages.

Chapter 3 unlocks the sensitivity code and presents 12 practical and effective ways to manage sensitivity. Our relationships define our lives, so Chapter 4 takes a detailed look at the people sensitives tend to attract into their lives or be attracted to. There is also advice on dealing with toxic relationships and the attachment trauma that sensitive people often experience as a result of craving intimacy while also paradoxically fearing getting close to anyone. Sensitive people can often feel overwhelmed by the demands of an insensitive, busy world, so Chapter 5 offers coping strategies. There is also a section here on the health issues and addictive behaviours that research shows gentle people tend to experience or use as coping mechanisms during sensitive times.

Chapter 6 revisits the classic sensitive traits of intuition and empathy, and shows how they have the potential to be supernormal powers. It also takes a brief look at recent research into the connection between sensitivity and so-called psychic abilities. Chapter 7 references the natural inclination towards the mystical that sensitive people often experience at some point in their lives. It explains why finding a spiritual perspective, or discovering meaning or a purpose in life and making a difference in the world is absolutely vital for sensitive people to thrive. The book concludes with an invitation to connect with kindred spirits and explore more ways for sensitives to unite and feel empowered.

If you are struggling to understand your sensitivity, or yearn to belong or be accepted by both yourself and others, there is much in this book to inform and guide – and hopefully inspire – you. If you long to make a difference in the world but have no idea how, *The Sensitivity Code* will give you the tools and motivation you need. You will discover that *now* is the perfect time for you to understand and cherish who you are and, by so doing, make your unique mark on the world.

The gentle power of now

In ancient times, people with heightened sensitivity traits were highly valued members of society. They were the shamans, oracles, poets, prophets and healers, alerting their peoples to possible danger or offering guidance and comfort. Artists, visionaries and philanthropists were venerated for the creativity, light and love they brought to the world. This isn't to say all sensitives are geniuses or saints, but their innate intuition and empathy typically gives them an overwhelming urge to find meaning, create connections, offer guidance, protect the underdog and ease the suffering of those in pain. Humanity once valued and respected sensitive traits, but today this recognition and respect has all but vanished.

This generation is now gripped by a wave of *Game of Thrones*-style materialism, corruption and narcissism. Sensitives have been gradually driven underground or condemned as weak, 'woo-woo' or irrelevant by a culture both on and offline that celebrates extroversion, egotism and ruthless competitiveness. As it is not in the natures of sensitives to stand up for themselves, their emotional intensity continues to be considered a form of weakness or a flaw in an increasingly conflicted world.

Everyone suffers when empathy, compassion, integrity and intuition are marginalised, and that is what is happening today.

Something urgently needs to be done to counteract that dark trend. Erasing the notion that sensitivity is a weakness, flaw or personality disorder is the first vital step. We need to see its strength and we also need to recognise that there is potential for sensitivity within us all. Yes, some of us are more naturally sensitive than others, but each one of us has sensitive traits and we need to be encouraged to value and express our milder or softer sides whenever they surface, not repress them.

This re-evaluation of sensitivity needs to start in childhood, with parents and teachers understanding that there is nothing wrong with children who experience life intensely. The worst advice you can ever give a sensitive child or person is to 'toughen up' or 'stop dreaming'. Likewise, in the workplace, we need to recognise the contribution of all personality types and not just celebrate the power of those who are driven and competitive. Indeed, the power of sensitives should be valued not just in the workplace but in every walk of life.

If you are sensitive, it's vital that you understand that *you* are the love, light and compassion that can bring healing to the world in these troubled times. And for the good of the planet, there is no more time to waste: *now* is definitely the right time for you to unleash the secret power of your sensitivity.

About the stories

The Sensitivity Code is first and foremost a book designed to empower sensitive people by offering information, advice and proven tools and strategies, but you will also notice that, alongside sharing my own life experiences, I have included a number of real stories from my readers. For the most part, these stories have been left unaltered, but I have changed names, and in some instances other details, to protect their identities. These stories are ones that people from all walks of life have sent me over the years and which they have generously given me permission to share. I have included these stories to add a sense of familiarity, because all too often highly sensitive individuals feel lonely and isolated, as if they are the only one who feels that way. I hope reading about the experiences of others will show you that you most certainly are not alone. You have many kindred spirits.

I also hope that reading the stories of other sensitive people will encourage you to get in touch with me. Details about how you can do so are in the 'Get in touch' section.

CHAPTER 1

Being Oh So Sensitive

As many as one in five people are highly sensitive. That's a lot of us. On top of that estimated number, factor in the reality that we can all be sensitive at times or feel overwhelmed by the world. Sensitivity, whether we want to acknowledge it or not, is inescapable.

But what exactly does it mean to be a sensitive person?

I feel you

Being sensitive means feeling things profoundly and for far longer than people generally consider to be 'normal'. It means being a deep thinker who contemplates every possible outcome of a situation. It means responding emotionally rather than rationally to events, environments, images, sounds, scents or the feelings and the moods, words and actions of others. It means sensing invisible or subtle details that others don't see or feel. It means being highly imaginative, empathetic beyond reason, intuitive beyond limits and having the ability to see similarities, patterns or the potential for connections rather than differences. When surrounded by too much external stimulation, required to multitask or placed under time pressure, it means feeling utterly overwhelmed or drained. Like a Jane Austen heroine (or Mr Bennet in *Pride and Prejudice*, regularly seeking solitude in his library, away from his bustling household) it means having an overwhelming compulsion to hide from the business of life to reflect and regroup in solitude. The self-isolation and social distancing imposed during the pandemic would not be difficult for sensitive souls to adjust too.

In essence, being sensitive means living your life with heightened awareness and emotional generosity. Around 20 percent of people live in a state of this constant high alert, and these are the people whom scientists and psychologists identify as highly sensitive. The rest of us don't identify strongly as highly sensitive, but we will still experience moments of acute sensitivity because we are all born with the innate *potential* to be sensitive.

The science of being sensitive

There is extensive research on the 20 percent of the population believed to be extremely sensitive and what we now know about them is helpful for understanding us all better.[6] Scientists use the technical term 'sensory-processing sensitivity' or SPS to describe sensitive traits in a person. Much of this research proves that being highly sensitive is innate or genetic and that highly responsive traits are important for our survival as a species, probably because highly sensitive people can pick up potential dangers or threats others might miss, and avert disaster.[7] This research has largely been pioneered by psychologist Dr Elaine Aron, and her studies all indicate that highly sensitive people are likely born, not made, which carries with it the possibility that it can be inherited from parents or from someone on the family tree. (If you want to find out more about Dr Aron's groundbreaking research, which I advise, do check out the resources section).

6 Aron, E. *et al.* (2012) 'Sensory processing sensitivity: A review in the light of evolution of biological responsibility.' *Personality and Social Psychology Review*, 16(3), 262–284.

7 Wolf, M. *et al.* (2008) 'Evolutionary emergence of responsive and unresponsive personalities.' *Proceeding of the National Academy of Sciences*, 105(41).

According to Aron, a child who is born highly sensitive is typically labelled a shy introvert by parents, carers and teachers. Their tendency is to withdraw when they feel overwhelmed by external stimuli, but this isn't necessarily because they are shy. It is often because they are experiencing sensory overload. It is a mistake to assume that high sensitivity and introversion are the same. They are not. It is possible to be sensitive and extroverted, as Aron's studies reveal that roughly 30 percent of highly sensitive people are extroverts in that they gain energy from social interaction.[8] For an extroverted sensitive person, spending too much time in withdrawal can make them lethargic and unmotivated.

It is early days yet, but growing numbers of scientists are interested in highly sensitive traits and the impact they have on a person's health and well-being. It has been found, for example, that the brains of people who are highly sensitive show far more activity in the areas associated with empathy and processing the difference between self and other than people without highly sensitive traits.[9] One study led by Aron and neuroscientist Bianca Acevedo showed that empathy was far more active in people who are highly sensitive when they were shown images of strong emotion compared to non-highly sensitive people also being shown images of strong emotion.[10] The same study demonstrated that the brains of highly sensitive people are strongly influenced by the moods of others.[11] It also seems the nervous system of the highly sensitive person has a lower tolerance for stress, hunger,

8 Aron, E. (2012) *Psychotherapy and the Highly Sensitive Person.* Routledge.

9 Pluess, M. and Belsky, J. (2013) 'Vantage Sensitivity: Individual differences in response to positive experience.' *Psychological Bulletin*, 139, 901–916.

10 Acevedo B. *et al.* (2014) 'The highly sensitive brain: An fMRI study of sensory processing sensitivity and response to others' emotions.' *Brain and Behavior*, July 4 (4) 580–594.

11 Acevedo B. *et al.* (2014) 'The highly sensitive brain: An fMRI study of sensory processing sensitivity and response to others' emotions.' *Brain and Behavior*, July 4 (4) 580–594.

noise and pain, which may explain why sensitives are more likely to be hyper-emotional, to notice and feel things other people don't and to suffer from stress-related health conditions.[12]

In addition, researchers believe that highly sensitive traits are often found in creative and artistic people and those drawn to the caring professions. Listening to music is likely to give them chills or make them feel overemotional.[13] On the downside, because they are so empathetic and easily overwhelmed by people and situations, they can be at an increased risk of stress and depression.[14] That's why it is essential for highly sensitive people or people going through sensitive times to pay close attention to self-care and their living and working environments. (More about how sensitive souls can protect themselves from stress can be found in Chapter 5: Living in an Overwhelming World.)

What is DOES?

To identify whether a person or a child is highly sensitive, psychologists from the American Psychological Association use a special identification or measurement scale, which asks simple questions to identify highly sensitive traits.[15] Examples include: Do the moods of others impact you? Are you aware of subtleties in your own environment? Do you often feel the need to withdraw? Are you easily overwhelmed? Are you highly sensitive to pain and hunger?

---

12 Pluess, M. *et al.* (2015) 'Sensory-processing sensitivity predicts treatment response to a school-based depression prevention program: Evidence of vantage sensitivity.' *Piers. Ind. Differ*, 82, 40–45.

13 Wallmark, Z. *et al.* (2018) 'Neurophysiological effects of trait empathy in music listening.' *Frontiers in Behavioral Neuroscience*, 12.

14 Homeberg J.R. *et al.* (2016) 'Sensory processing sensitivity and serotonin gene variance: Insights into mechanisms shaping environmental sensitivity.' *Neuroscience and Biobehavioural reviews*, 71, 472–483.

15 www.hsperson.com/research/measurement-scales-for-researchers

However, according to Aron, all highly sensitive people, whether introvert or extrovert, possess four main traits, which can easily be remembered by the acronym DOES:[16]

> D: Depth of processing – highly sensitive people analyse everything, considering every possible scenario before making a decision.
> O: Overstimulation – they can easily get overpowered by sights, sounds and the environment they are in.
> E: Empathy and emotional responsiveness – they don't just identify with what others are feeling, they feel it themselves.
> S: Sensitivity to subtleties – they hear, see, feel and sense tiny details that others easily miss.

The implication of Aron's research is that the remaining 80 percent of the population do not possess the four defining DOES traits. I am not a scientist or a psychologist, but I have been writing about and collecting stories from sensitive people for decades now. I have come to the conclusion that although the remaining 80 percent may not display DOES traits as consistently or acutely as a person who is born highly sensitive, they still have the potential to manifest highly sensitive traits. Sensitivity can be triggered in anyone, whether diagnosed highly sensitive or not, by traumatic events, such as bereavement, heartbreak or other life crises, or simply by a sudden and unexpected desire to go within and find deeper meaning.

Am I highly sensitive?

My preference is to avoid diagnosis because it suggests that being highly sensitive is unnatural or unusual when it isn't. It is perfectly

---

16 www.hsperson.com/research/published-articles

natural, just as being musically gifted is perfectly natural. If some-one is born with a musical gift they do not need to be diagnosed by a psychologist as 'highly musical'. Having said that, sometimes it can help to know where you are on the sensitivity spectrum. With this in mind, I have created a self-help tool: a sensitivity scale that you can use as a gauge, or that you can use for someone you know to help them understand themselves better.

Listed below are the most common highly sensitive traits, or traits that psychologists believe identify a person as being highly sensitive. They have been reframed as questions to which you can answer yes or no. If you aren't sure of your answer then the answer is no. The higher you score, the more likely it is that you are a highly sensitive person. If you don't score on every trait, this doesn't mean you aren't sensitive and won't ever be, it means that your potential for high sensitivity isn't fully activated or triggered at this present moment.

Note: This scale is NOT meant to diagnose high sensitivity or exclude it, and is not a substitute for testing by psychologists and scientists. Bear in mind, too, that no questionnaire can cover all bases, and if you recognise yourself in the stories shared in this book, then you can consider yourself sensitive.

1. Do you sense or feel what other people are feeling without them having to explain?
2. Do you feel things deeply and for longer than other people do?
3. When you were a child did people call you sensitive or an old soul?
4. Do you have a rich inner life? Do you have a vivid imagination? Are you a 'head in the clouds' kind of person, prone to daydreaming?
5. Do you regularly need quiet time alone to withdraw or recharge?

6. Do you find it deeply distressing seeing violence on screen or images of cruelty?
7. Do you find it easy to give to or help others but hard to let people get close to you?
8. Do you find loud noises, strong scents and bright lights distressing? Are you easily startled?
9. Do you feel deeply moved by or drawn to music, creativity and the arts?
10. Do you get stressed and find it impossible to concentrate when you are hungry?
11. Do you find it extremely difficult to manage physical pain?
12. Do you take ages to make any kind of decision, even relatively simple ones like choosing what to eat on a menu?
13. Do busy and crowded places make you feel overwhelmed?
14. Are you extremely sensitive to any kind of negativity?
15. Do you have a strong sense of integrity and ethics?
16. Do other people find it easy to open up to you and often say they feel better after spending time with you?
17. Do you pick up on subtle changes in mood?
18. Do you pick up on subtle changes in the environment?
19. Are you extremely sensitive to the effects of caffeine, alcohol or any kind of stimulant?
20. Do high-pressure situations, especially ones in which you are being observed or which require public speaking, make you panic?
21. Do you panic when under time pressure or when you have too many things to do at once?
22. Do you prefer to plan and schedule your time? Does the unexpected, visiting new places or meeting new people derail you?

23. Do you struggle to love yourself or feel that you are good enough to be loved?

24. Do you typically place the well-being of others above your own?

25. Do your partners and loved ones often find it hard to understand you?

26. Do you find it very hard, if not impossible, to recover when others judge, criticise, betray or lie to you?

27. Have you ever turned to food, alcohol or addictive or compulsive behaviour to cope with your sensitivity?

28. Are you drawn to environmental or charitable causes?

29. Do you have a great affinity for animals and nature?

30. Do you often feel that you are an outsider or that you don't belong?

31. Do you long to know what the meaning and purpose of your life is? Likewise, do you long to make a difference in the world?

32. Do you describe yourself as a spiritual person or believe in unseen forces and energies?

What did you score?

If you answered yes to more than 20 questions, then you are very likely a highly sensitive person.

If you answered yes to between 10 and 20 questions, then you are very likely a sensitive person.

If you answered yes to less than ten questions, then you are probably feeling sensitive right now or going through sensitive times. (Be aware, though, that even answering yes to just a few questions, and experiencing those sensitive traits acutely, could mean that you are extremely sensitive.)

If nothing resonated at all then you are not highly sensitive or going through sensitive times.

The spectrum of sensitivity

Whatever you scored, the potential for sensitivity is within you. Everyone can be sensitive at certain times in their lives. Sensitivity exists on a spectrum. At the top end of the spectrum are people who are born sensitive – people who would probably be diagnosed by psychologists as a highly sensitive person or HSP. Here's Hayley's story.

When I was growing up, my closest friends were my two dogs. Sometimes I would come home from school and the love I felt for them as they bounded to see me with tails wagging was so powerful that I would burst into tears. I was a loner at school and was perhaps the only child who enjoyed rainy days, because it meant there was no outside playtime and I could go into the library and quietly read a book. To this day I love picture books. I lose myself in them.

I'm all grown up now and less of a loner, but I still only have a few close friends and that is more than enough for me. I invest myself fully in my friendships and simply couldn't take on anyone else. It would be too draining. I work as a nurse and love my job, but if I am observed by a doctor or a senior nurse I go to pieces. I do go to parties but only because it is expected of me and I don't want to offend, not because I enjoy them. I am always the first to leave. I enjoy quiet time alone. If I don't recharge regularly or get enough alone time, I get headaches and stomach pains.

I live my life on high alert. It's hard to describe the hows or whys, but I am aware of literally everything. It is easy for me to read people and to put myself in their shoes. The moods of others impact me deeply and I often think it is my fault if they feel low. I can't pass a beggar in the street without wanting to cry and emptying my purse for them. If I watch anything on TV, I can identify with the characters completely, but if there is violence or cruelty of any kind I just can't bear to watch. Many a time I have walked out of a cinema viewing.

I love to help people and to listen to them talk. Being liked is important to me, but I often worry that I have offended others. I play conversations over and over again in my mind. I loathe crowds with a passion and even feel anxious if people sit too close to me in a restaurant. I can't travel on the Tube because my personal space is invaded. I walk or drive everywhere.

Hayley, 34

At the other end of the spectrum are people who appear to have zero sensitivity. They exhibit insensitive, ruthless, aggressive, narcissistic traits. According to the *Diagnostic and Statistical Manual of Mental Disorders*, fifth edition, it is estimated that around one percent of people are narcissists or have a condition known as narcissistic personality disorder (NPD), although not all narcissists are present for diagnosis, so experts believe the number may be far higher. This zero-empathy approach to life could be innate, but more research needs to be done and this certainly is not the place to diagnose a mental disorder.[17] Having said that, the strong likelihood is that narcissists, unlike sensitives, are made rather than born. Their potential for empathy is squeezed out of them by some kind of trauma, such as physical or emotional abuse in early childhood, or perhaps by excessive indulgence of their every whim, so they grow up feeling that the world revolves around only them. This is known as the golden child syndrome.

---

17 Yakeley, J. (2018) 'Current understanding of narcissism and narcissistic personality disorder.' *BJPsych Advances*, 24(5), 305–315.

Here's an extract from the diary of a man recently diagnosed with narcissistic personality disorder, who wrote to me after he read one of my books. It makes for chilling reading.

> My mother used to hit me when she was drunk and I was abused by my uncle. Home life was hell and I couldn't wait to leave and live life on my terms when I turned 17. If I can't control or manipulate people to do exactly what I want, or to give me what I need to feel good about myself, I discard them. They are bad people in my mind and of no use to me. I believe I am more intelligent and charismatic than everyone else and so it is my way or the highway. Follow my agenda and if I decide to change the agenda at any point, don't question me. I am always right. I hate being alone. I need to be surrounded by other people all the time but I don't let any of them get emotionally close. Popularity, money, sex and power are what matter most to me. As for feelings, I don't really have any. I'm numb and find it easy to pretend to feel something for someone else to get what I want in return.
>
> John, 44

NPD is a medical condition and outside the scope of this book. However, it is important to mention the condition here, not only because it sits right at the bottom of the sensitivity scale, but also because opposites attract. I have found in my research that highly sensitive people are often drawn to or become victims of people with narcissistic traits. (More about the destructive co-dependent dance between a narcissist and a sensitive soul, and the way forward, in Chapter 4: Heartfelt.)

So, if around 20 percent of us are born highly sensitive and up to 6 percent may be dangerously low on the sensitivity spectrum, that leaves (at least) around 74 percent of us who may travel up and down the spectrum of sensitivity during the course of our lives. Typically, stressful events or times of great change, such as heartbreak, divorce, job loss or bereavement, can send people who may not necessarily identify as highly sensitive spiralling towards high sensitivity.

> Growing up, I was never a 'crybaby'. I was always together. It took a lot for me to cry or feel emotional. I was head girl and I'd be the one everyone relied on. Then after I had my first child, I completely changed. I cry very easily now but they aren't always sad tears. It's like I'm catching up on all the crying I didn't do as a child. I feel and sense things more deeply now, too.
>
> Mary, 24

> My heart burst wide open after my wife died. We had been married for 33 happy years. Suddenly I became aware of all this empathy inside me that I hadn't known existed before. I started to see beyond the surface of things. I didn't immediately believe what I saw. I never used to have time for my friends when they were going through relationship break-ups or rough times. I just told them time would heal or there were plenty of other fish in the sea. I would help them practically if I could, but I couldn't see the point of listening. Now I see the point completely. My broken heart has taught me to listen, really listen, and how much value there is in simply being there for other people.
>
> Philip, 64

> I'm in no way an emotional or sensitive person. In fact, my family playfully call me a 'stone'. It's not that I don't care, it's just that I am a very practical and pragmatic person. I do have one Achilles heel though. Whenever I hear beautiful music, especially opera, I feel the music

and singing very intensely. It never fails to bring tears to my eyes, my heart beats loudly and I am lost in emotions I didn't know I had.

Sajidah, 47

Whatever your sensitive feelings are triggered by, the advice in Chapter 3 will help you transform them into opportunities for personal growth.

Research into sensitive traits and the fact that the genetic coding for sensitivity has survived evolution, suggests that the potential for sensitivity is within us all, and although scientists debate whether this is for evolutionary advantage, there is always the possibility that it may even be necessary. I believe it is. To risk paraphrasing the immortal John Lennon in his song 'Imagine', which resonates so powerfully with sensitive souls, just visualise a world where there is only peace.

Although I score highly on the sensitivity scale, I don't actually meet all the criteria. For example, even though I get extremely nervous, I love public speaking – something many sensitive people find traumatic. And sometimes I am far more sensitive to the moods of others than at other times. My sensitivity to them depends on what is going on in my life. I am usually observant and considerate, but on occasion I miss the point entirely. I have been told I can be unintentionally blunt and thoughtless. I also don't get overstimulated by caffeine – indeed, coffee houses have become my retreat.

This doesn't mean that I am not a sensitive or highly sensitive person. It just means that I am human, and although I'm naturally inclined towards high sensitivity, I go up and down the scale like everyone else. I've also found that as I get older I am better able to manage my sensitivity, even though Aron's research finds the opposite is often true and people get more, not less, sensitive with age. Despite this, I'm convinced that if I did an HSP test with a psychologist now, I would score much lower than if I had done the test 20 years ago; but, as stated earlier, this doesn't mean I am no longer a sensitive person. It means I have done my research and found ways to manage my sensitivity and transform it into a strength. I will share those strategies with you in this book.

I am including the story of my childhood and my journey towards becoming aware of my sensitive traits. I'm doing this not because my story is particularly special, but so you can see where I am coming from and how the odds were stacked against me. I trust it will reassure you that however impossible it may seem at times, whatever your background and whatever your age, you can transform being sensitive into a strength. I hope that reading my journey will encourage you to reflect honestly on your own childhood and your own journey. Hindsight can be a great teacher and self-development tool for everyone, especially for sensitive souls.

Sensitive voices

'Theresa, you are just too sensitive for your own good.'

'You've really got to toughen up.'

'Stop being such a wuss.'

I heard this kind of thing a lot when I was growing up. It always made me feel like there was something pathetic and wrong about me. I believed I was an ineffective 'crybaby' and that my sensitivity was bad, something I had to overcome.

One memory is forever with me. I was nine years old and I was sitting on the bus to school. I was feeling very proud of myself because I had finally faced my fears and mustered up the courage to go and get a seat upstairs, and I didn't have just any seat – I had the front seat, where the cool kids often got to sit. I felt a bit of an imposter sitting there, because even at such a tender age I didn't in any way think of myself as someone cool. It felt glorious seeing the world for the first time by myself from such a height. I felt on top of the world, literally and emotionally. Then, in a flash my joy turned to abject horror as a bird smacked into the window and then slid down it, most likely to be crushed under the wheels of the bus.

A couple of boys sitting in the seats next to me found the whole episode thrilling but the sudden, senseless and violent end of that bird traumatised every cell of my body. Tears slid uncontrollably down my cheeks and I placed my hands over my ears in a futile attempt to block out the laughing reaction to the incident of the boys. I couldn't drown out hearing one of them say that the bird was probably stuck to the wheel of the bus, going around and around, even singing the nursery rhyme as he did it. It was grotesque. Another said that it might still be half alive and limping in pain on the road with its head on back to front. They discussed every possible gruesome scenario with glee. To this day I can remember in vivid detail the chill I felt and my total lack of comprehension that people could delight in suffering in this way. All day at school my mind kept returning over and over again to the bird and what had or might have happened to it.

After school, when I was on the bus returning home, I didn't dare go upstairs and could hardly bring myself to look out of the window. But when the bus got to the spot where the incident had happened, I felt weirdly compelled to look. I saw it lying crushed in a pile of red feathers. Car after car had run over it at the side of the road. It was like an arrow to my heart. For the next few days, weeks and even months, my thoughts compulsively returned to the violent and lonely death of that bird. I didn't ride on the upper deck of the school bus for at least another year.

This incident wasn't unusual for me. To this day, any kind of suffering, particularly when it involves animals, tears at my heart and gives me nightmares. At the age of ten I became a vegetarian after watching a documentary at school about the lambing industry. The teacher made me watch it even though I hid my head in my hands and repeatedly asked to go to the bathroom to be sick.

At school there was very low tolerance for my sensitive nature from teachers and there certainly wasn't any understanding from my classmates. I was relentlessly teased for crying or overreacting to things. If I didn't understand something the teacher was trying to tell me, I would start to cry. If friends didn't want to play with me, I would cry some more. I would obsess over every single thing anyone said to me. Hardly surprising then that I was a lonely and friendless child as everybody must have felt they had to walk on eggshells around me. When things got too much my dear mum would comfort me as my tears just kept on flowing. She told me over and over again that I needed to be less sensitive and not take everything to heart. I didn't know how else to be. I lived life through the lens of my heart. I couldn't separate myself from anyone or anything. Lacking the ability to set boundaries with other people, I didn't know where I ended and other people began.

Unsurprisingly, given my sensitivity, I struggled to fit in when I was growing up in the loud and vibrant 1970s, a decade not known for its subtlety. I was unbearably sensitive and shy. There were countless anxious school lunchtimes when I clutched my plastic blue tray and agonised about whether or not anyone would sit with me. They rarely did. PE sessions were another torture as, of course, the team leaders picked everyone but me for their team. I don't blame them. I didn't have the competitive and confident streak needed to win. My lessons were mostly spent sitting on a table alone and break times were largely spent hiding from my exuberant peers.

Fitting in wasn't made easier by my family's poverty-stricken, alternative lifestyle. I grew up in a family of sensitives and professional psychics, and back then New Age was not enjoying the revival it is seeing today. People viewed it with great suspicion. We never seemed to settle in one place long enough to call it home, and then things got even worse when the relationship between my parents irretrievably broke down. After their separation, my father was absent from my life and my mother constantly depressed. All this building tension in both my school and my home life added to my ever increasing sense of rejection and isolation.

As a teenager, my sensitivity just deepened. Hardest of all to deal with, though, was my habit of breaking into spontaneous tears and my tendency to run away from situations that made me feel exposed. I remember my first Saturday job. I was about 15 at the time. It was working in a newsagent and after some basic training I was given the responsibility of operating the till at the back of the store. I dreaded any kind of customer query in case I couldn't direct them to the right place but more than that I dreaded them actually purchasing something. The till felt unbearably complicated and I worried that I would give the wrong change. Of course, that is exactly what happened. A customer returned to the newsagent saying I had given them the wrong change. The supervisor came towards me and I could see the customer shaking their head and holding out the change in their hand. Panicked, I burst into tears and ran out of the store before either of them could speak to me. I am an honest person and could not cope with the shame of being accused of stealing. It was only later in the evening that I found out that the customer was scrupulously honest. I had given them too much change and not too little. Of course, I was fired for leaving the till!

As crowds made me feel uncomfortable and confused, life at a huge and underperforming comprehensive girls' school was a daily ordeal, so I left as soon as I could, at the age of 16, with virtually no qualifications. It's not that I was lazy, lacking in ability or didn't want to learn, I just struggled to concentrate in class. There was too much chaos, voices, sounds and distraction. My end-of-term school reports were disappointing. My teachers didn't offer much hope for me career wise. I was still eager to learn though but on my own terms in peace and quiet. So I got a part-time job as a care assistant in an old people's home and carried on with my education via a correspondence or home study course.

In many ways, working part-time in a care home was an ideal fit, because caring for and helping others comes totally naturally to me. I also basked in the peaceful routine and order of life there. However, there are challenges for anyone working in an environment where poor health is prevalent and death a frequent event, and particularly for someone who is sensitive, because research now shows that the area of the brain associated with empathy is more active in sensitive people. I sensed and felt the pain of the residents and the grief of their relatives acutely, as if it were my own.

On more than one occasion, I was present when a resident passed away. I sensed a world of unseen emotions and sensations that to this day I still can't explain. It was a tough and often heart-breaking job, but like many sensitive people I gave the appearance of coping. Looking back, I'm not entirely sure how I did it, given what I know now about being sensitive.

It was during this period in my life that I also developed an intense craving for solitude. Time alone to regroup after work or any kind of stimulation was as essential for me as food and drink. I needed lengthy periods of reflection and withdrawal, and because of this craving for alone time and my affinity with all things spiritual, I seriously considered becoming a nun. I even spent a few weeks in a convent retreat to contemplate this option.

During my retreat, the gentle rhythm of prayers and solitude felt like bliss. I believe many people drawn to the contemplative life may well be highly sensitive. They need silence, simplicity and solitude to function at their peak. I learned many useful coping tools while I was there, but perhaps the most valuable lesson of all was that contentment does not come from material things or 'stuff'. It comes from within. Somehow, though, that life lesson was easier to learn and live by within the convent. It took me several decades to learn to apply it fully in my everyday life.

Even though I was truly drawn to a life of contemplation, by the end of the retreat I realised it was something I could not do. Yes,

I was daunted by the world, but I knew I didn't wish to withdraw from it completely. I wanted to make my mark in some way and make a difference, even if I didn't yet know how to do that.

And all that reflective time and home-alone study worked for me, because much to my own surprise – and the surprise of everyone, especially my former school teachers – I gained the required results for a place at King's College, University of Cambridge, to read Theology and English. I was elated and honoured to be offered a place at such an esteemed establishment, but inevitably, once I got used to the idea, my insecurities returned. Would I ever feel at home there? Although I loved studying at King's, it soon became evident that I wasn't going to fit in there either. I didn't have the money or confidence to hold my own with the privately educated and, back then, largely male-dominated 'elite' studying there. I was, yet again, in my own mind, an outsider and an imposter.

Many times, I felt as if I was the university's social experiment or poverty poster girl. I would hide in my room, unable to muster the confidence to eat with my fellow students in the magnificent dining hall. It was just too overwhelming, and I didn't feel I had any right to be there. Instead, I would sit anxiously in my room with a packet of crisps and a bottle of water, only tiptoeing outside when I had lectures or tutorials to attend. I didn't participate in university social life at all. It wasn't that I didn't want to, it was that I didn't know how to behave. I recalled all those times at junior and senior school when my peers had called me strange. I had taken all their taunting seriously and was absolutely convinced there was something wrong with me and I did not belong. I was the outcast, dressing entirely in black every single day so as not to draw any attention to myself.

Paradoxically, though, I found a 'home' of sorts on the stage and was cast in many student plays, perhaps because it was easier for me to pretend to be someone else. On stage I could be the kind of person I wanted to be. I somehow kept going in this incoherent, conflicted, insecure way for three years, until I graduated, but nerves and lack of funding prevented me from even attending my own graduation. My name was called out but I wasn't there to collect my certificate. It was mailed to me instead. I got my degree, but I was the invisible student.

With such low self-esteem and hypersensitivity to everyone and everything, I was poorly equipped to deal with life in the real world. I was an accident waiting to happen and made some ill-judged career and relationship choices. Instead of using my degree to get a job that suited my level of intelligence I applied for jobs I was overqualified for. Instead of going out with men who treated me as their equal, I dated men who were narcissists or who needed me to take care of them and do 100 percent of the giving in the relationship, because I didn't think I deserved any better. This disfunction limped on for a good few years. Sometimes it really did feel as if I was too sensitive for the world, as I simply couldn't cope with everyday life. My one rock was my mum, which meant that the trauma of her death to cancer in my mid-twenties was soul-shattering. My heart was in pieces and so was my life. I had always hoped that when I grew up and became an adult, I would somehow grow some self-confidence and leave my insecurities behind with my childhood. However, by my late twenties, I was more sensitive and uncertain about myself and my place in the world than ever.

There were some positive developments. I did find a few friends, but perhaps looking back they found me. My willingness to always listen, not share my own problems and my ability to people-please and be as helpful and as undemanding as possible made me an attractive proposition. I just didn't set any boundaries in my friendships. It wasn't all one way, though, because even though I gave more than I received from my friends at time, I enjoyed the way being needed by other people made me feel.

Another positive step for me was that I began to understand myself better and what kind of career suited me. Being sensitive to moods and environments I realised that working in an office or big publishing company wasn't for me. I needed my independence. I trained to be a teacher and spent a year or two working as a secondary school English teacher. I loved teaching but it wasn't the ideal fit, as I found myself unable to switch off from the needs of my pupils and utterly drained at the end of each day. Eventually, I started doing some freelance journalism and, in the process, discovered a passion for informing, teaching and healing others through words. Yet despite this newfound passion to inspire others I still felt like an outsider, as if I wasn't meant for this life. Given my personal and academic background, I wrote numerous features and then went on to write books about health in mind, body and spirit but behind the scenes I was still suffering from crippling low self-esteem and relationship struggles as well as financial insecurity. I was a full-blown cliché of the wounded healer, hiding behind my desk and my words.

So, I limped along in this muddled way trying to fit in and find ways to disguise my sensitivity and insecurities. There were highlights along the way. I did manage, eventually, to fall in love with a wonderful man who treated me with respect, and we got married. I was also blessed with two healthy children. There were bouts of postnatal depression after the births of both my children, but alongside that there were also moments of pure joy.

Time flew by as I raised my children and tended to their every need, and before long they were young children due to start school. Having felt so alienated at school myself you can imagine how anxious I felt about sending them to school. Letting go sounds easy, but like so many things in my life, what should have been easy was, once again, incredibly hard. I suffered from severe and debilitating separation anxiety. I had to learn the long and hard way that children are a gift loaned to you and that good parenting is about letting go gradually. It took me a while to assimilate that vital life lesson, but once I began to learn it, I was finally able to immerse myself in my writing.

With feelings of excitement and renewed enthusiasm, I put my pen – or should I say keyboard – where my heart was and decided to finally do something about the countless stories I had been sent by people during my years as spiritual researcher. The material was so personal and illuminating I could clearly see their stories gathered together in book form. As these sensitive souls continued to get in touch with me to talk about how they felt, it became apparent that many of them displayed remarkably similar personality traits to mine.

Many of them told me that they were also sensitive and naturally tuned into the moods of others or the environment they were in. They could not abide cruelty in any form and felt a deep emotional connection with nature and animals. For some, simply reading distressing news reports or watching them on the TV was enough to trigger feelings of despair and distress because their empathy was so very deep. Many told me that they had always felt drawn to healing, helping or inspiring others, even though they themselves suffered from low self-confidence or relationship problems and had no idea how to translate their desire to make a positive difference in the world into a reality. Some mentioned how much they hated or felt alienated at school and how for most of their lives they felt like they were outsiders. Others talked about sensing atmospheres and the feelings of others, or simply knowing things without knowing how they knew.

Most of them did not say they were sensitive but reading their stories and insights was like looking directly into my own heart, my own soul. I wasn't alone or the only one going through all this any more. For the first time in forever I actually felt like I belonged. I was coming home. I started to do extensive research into sensitive personalities and discovered it was a genetic trait. Most significantly for me, though, given the nature of the spiritual books I was writing, I discovered that sensitive people tend to believe, as I do, that there is transformative (perhaps eternal, if you are spiritually inclined) power in love, kindness and gentleness. Sensitive people just need to learn how to harness their sensitivity so it can empower them and become a healing force in the world.

If only I had had access to this kind of insight and information before about being a sensitive person. It would have helped me understand myself better and cope with my sensitivity and unsettling feelings of always being different or out of place when I was growing up. Simply finding out that I was not alone, and that what I had always regarded as a flaw or weakness could become my greatest strength, was not just reassuring, it was life-changing. I also realised that placing too much emphasis on being sensitive wasn't always helpful, because it implied that being over sensitive was something out of the ordinary, when in fact there is potential for sensitivity within us all. It also didn't allow for the possibility that as we progress through life we evolve. Our hearts grow in wisdom and power.

Writing this book has finally enabled me to address the issue of being sensitive directly and to the general reader, rather than cloaking it in spiritual or New Age terminology or referring to it as a condition to be diagnosed, as I have felt the need to do before.

I am in no doubt that you are reading this book for a reason. In my humble opinion, you are meant to read it. And when a sensitive person lets their intuition guide them in this way, they become a light to ignite and inspire greater sensitivity in others. When you have the courage to understand and celebrate your sensitivity, others can catch a glimpse of a more compassionate world.

At many times in my life, I have tried to be someone I am not, and my sensitive nature has led to feelings of isolation and confusion. I haven't always trusted my sensitive instincts and I am still a work in progress (as my *Under the Skin* interview experience, discussed in the introduction, demonstrated), but now that I'm most definitely in my mature years I finally know who I am and what I need to do. I hope it doesn't take you as long to celebrate who you are as it did me. I want to empower gentle souls to believe they are a force that can change the world for the better. I've had my fair share of challenges and knock-backs living as a sensitive in an insensitive world, but along the way I have refined some highly effective self-help tools to manage my traits and turn them to my advantage. These I will reveal later in this book.

What's your story?

It's likely that your story will be similar to mine in terms of often feeling emotionally overwhelmed or that you don't belong, but one thing is for sure – the story of your sensitive life will be unique. We are all unique miracles of DNA and we each experience life in our own individual way. There are many books and resources now for the so-called 'highly sensitive', and this is a very positive development – far better than being ignored or ridiculed – but before we move towards the heart of this book, never forget that sensitive people are all individuals.

The moment you start putting sensitive people into a special category by defining the characteristics required to qualify, you create a 'them and us' mentality. It's also the moment that being sensitive becomes something different or 'other', when it really isn't. Never forget that we all have the potential for sensitivity, and the capacity for empathy, intuition, kindness and gentleness it brings.

Going through sensitive times at some point in your life is all part of what makes you a human being with a beating heart. I hope reading my story has encouraged you to reflect on the story of your own beating heart, as well as your past and what brought you here.

Figuring yourself out

This chapter has briefly explored the science of being sensitive, diagnostic criteria for HSPs and how helpful a diagnosis really is. I have also shared my journey to greater self-awareness, including some of the challenges I have faced and how long it has taken me to finally make sense of my sensitivity, so you can reflect on your own story.

There's a reason it has taken me so long. Despite a remarkable ability to understand what makes other people tick, sensitive people often don't understand themselves at all. They tend to lack self-awareness and downplay or dismiss their strengths. I know this to be true from all the sensitive stories I have read and all the sensitive people I have spoken to over these last 15 or so years. Most of them lack self-belief or doubt themselves, even though they are sharing profound insights and stories and express beautiful things. I also know it to be true because it has taken me so very long to figure myself out and see my own value – and I'm still working on it.

Coming up...

Chapter 2 digs deeper beneath the surface and reveals the hidden psychology of sensitivity. It explores the reasons why so many sensitives don't understand themselves or value the advantages or strengths of gentleness. It outlines the pros and cons – the benefits and the blind spots – of living a sensitive life, so that you can adapt the self-help strategies offered in Chapter 3 to help you cope with your own challenges and, most importantly of all, finally and fully acknowledge the true blessings of being a sensitive soul.

CHAPTER 2

Blind Spots and Blessings

Sensitive people often have the uncanny ability to read others remarkably well. More often than not their intuition about what others are feeling, thinking, fearing or desiring is spot on. However, they aren't nearly as accurate when it comes to understanding themselves and their own feelings, thoughts, fears and desires. Indeed, their lack of self-awareness is quite simply astonishing given how perceptive they are about others.

I often find myself clearly sensing what is going on for others, what their problems are and knowing what is best for them. But then when it comes to issues that need resolving in my own life, I am clueless, often paralysed with indecision.

In hindsight, I can see that many of my struggles have been directly related to a lack of self-knowledge. For example, in my early adult life I remember gamely tagging along with groups of my peers to crowded music festivals or packed nightclubs with loud music, lots of smoke and drugs, and feeling that I needed to do this sort of thing to 'fit in'. I quietly loathed every minute, but pretended that I was having the time of my life. In the early hours of the morning I would get back to wherever home was at the time and spend hours fighting back tears, while obsessively washing the smoke and alcohol smells out of my hair and clothes.

It is the same with my friendships. I love people. When I'm with them I give them my full attention. I genuinely want to listen. I love to help them if I can. But as well as craving closeness, I also need plenty of space. My friends always seem to want more of my time than I feel comfortable giving. Again, because I thought it was expected of me and I feared upsetting or disappointing anyone, in the past I ended up oversharing and being taken over or feeling controlled by my friendships. Intimate relationships were a similar struggle – I needed them but was reluctant to get too close, wanting companionship and space at the same time.

Not understanding myself, I felt like a conflicted outsider or oddball – as many sensitive people do – so learning about my sensitive personality, and that it wasn't a fault but normal, was magical. Finding out that other people felt this way too and were silently struggling like me, and that being sensitive could be reframed as a strength rather than a weakness, was life-changing.

Once they feel comfortable in their own skins, sensitive people have the ability to bring healing and do remarkable good in the world. The only thing holding them back is not understanding or valuing who they really are.

This chapter will help erase the self-knowledge barrier that routinely blocks sensitive souls from thriving. In the words of Aristotle, knowing yourself is the beginning of all wisdom. For people who are sensitive, self-knowledge is key. It is the root of all their power. Understanding yourself is a crucial step towards personal growth and fulfilment and absolutely essential if you are to transform your sensitivity from a perceived flaw into a strength.

Know your blind spots

For the first three decades of my life, I felt adrift. I knew I wanted to help people, so I became a nurse. I finished my training and went to work on the hospital wards. I felt I had found my vocation. But over time, seeing human suffering so up close and personal gradually took a heavy toll on my emotional and physical health. I gained way too much weight and constantly suffered from colds and bouts of anxiety. I felt deeply how unfair and cruel life can be. I watched patients die of loneliness because their family didn't want to visit them, not because of the disease they had been diagnosed with. I saw children die before their parents. I had a nervous breakdown. I left the nursing profession and am now a medical researcher, which suits me better. It's a great shame though, as I was a very good nurse and it was the most rewarding job. I just wish I had been tougher at the time. If only I had known about being highly sensitive, I could have found ways to protect myself better and stayed in the job I loved.

Mary, 35

We all know what blind spots are when driving. They occur when vehicles are driving very close to us or objects are there but we can't see them in our mirrors. If we don't take the possibility of those blind spots into account and physically check for them by turning our heads, the chances of having an accident substantially increase. Similarly, psychological blinds spots are aspects of ourselves that we can't 'see'. They are patterns of behaviour that we are not fully aware of, and we need a shift of perspective to recognise them. They have become so much a part of who we are and how we respond that they impact all the choices we make.

Your blind spots are your unconscious fears, habits, patterns, needs, truths and motives, among other things. In essence, they comprise what you can't see about yourself. They contain what is hidden deep within you – things that, at some point in your life and for whatever reason, you didn't wish to acknowledge, so you buried them. Perhaps you felt ashamed, or that you would be criticised, or that to reveal your true feelings would be dangerous in some way. Perhaps you thought you needed to conceal a perceived personality flaw or weakness. Whatever the reason you buried them, these aspects of yourself operate automatically in the dark. You don't feel safe or comfortable acknowledging them, and you don't want others to see them either.

This chapter is all about shining a bright light on who you truly are, both the shadowy aspects and the empowering sides of your personality. Not being fully aware of who you really are is potentially just as dangerous as not seeing something close when you are driving. To become more self-aware and make better choices moving forward, you need to be able to distinguish between when you are making choices consciously and when you are unconsciously operating from your blind spots.

Blind spots often have their roots in the beliefs or responses you learned as a child to help cope with your innate sensitivity or deal with specific challenges or traumas. So, most will have formed as a protective mechanism during your vulnerable childhood years, but over time, as your life moved forward, those beliefs or responses no longer served your best interests. You've grown out of them but they have become so ingrained that they remain a part of you. Beliefs or responses can become so unconscious that you persist in them regardless, even though they no longer protect you and now block your chances of success and happiness in life.

I have noticed that many sensitive people have had challenging or traumatic childhoods. Many were bullied either at home or at school for their gentle responses, which caused them to become ashamed of who they really were and contributed to their feelings of low self-worth. However, it is important to point out that not all sensitive souls had tough childhoods. Some had positive experiences in their early years but still struggle as adults to manage their sensitivity in an insensitive world.

Every sensitive person is unique, but the most common blind spots I've learned about from my research and the stories sent to me by gentle people are outlined below. Once you become fully aware of your own potential blind spots, you can use the tools and techniques outlined in Chapter 3 to take positive action. As you read, bear in mind that not all blind spots are negative. Just because you have buried something about yourself or consigned it to the shadows does not necessarily mean it is bad. It simply means there's something about yourself that you aren't aware of and haven't learned to acknowledge… yet.

What lies beneath

I hope that reading about the following blind spots, listed in no particular order, will offer valuable insights into your own unconscious beliefs, so you can establish a firm foundation of greater self-awareness to build on from here.

Vulnerability is weakness

At school, I used to bury my head in my books and avoid any kind of eye contact with my teachers whenever they asked the class a question. Even if I was sure I knew the right answer, I couldn't risk being wrong and getting criticised. On the rare occasion I was invited to contribute or speak up, it was pure torture. My reports consistently said that the school wanted me to participate more in class discussions. On one occasion my mother came home from a meeting at school and said that the head teacher had no idea who I really was, as I was so quiet.

Mark, 26

I left university with a first-class honours degree and went straight into a six-month internship with a major company. Everyone there had high expectations of me. But I felt completely out of my depth. I pretended I knew what I was doing, but I didn't have a clue, really, and made a complete mess of things. Unsurprisingly, when I finished the internship, I wasn't hired. Looking back, the outcome could have been very different if I had been honest from the start and had had the courage to simply ask for help and advice instead of pretending everything was perfect.

Jo, 33

At some point in your life, the message that being vulnerable is a weakness became ingrained. Perhaps you were called a 'crybaby' at school by your classmates, or maybe an overly strict parent, teacher or authority figure instilled feelings of great fear in you whenever you felt uncertain. Or perhaps there's no reason at all and you have simply always struggled to speak up and express yourself.

Whatever the cause, over time you have learned to mask your true feelings or go into hiding whenever you feel threatened, vulnerable or exposed in any way. When you were a child, you probably thought that once you grew up you would no longer feel vulnerable, but even if you are not a sensitive person, it's worth remembering that to be alive is to be vulnerable. Part of growing up is finding the courage to reveal and express your authentic self to others and to risk uncertainty, criticism and rejection. There are no guarantees in life, whatever kind of personality you have. The tools and techniques in the next chapter will help you find the courage to shed your fears of being seen and heard for who you truly are.

Failure is not an option

I'm a copy editor and I fully immerse myself in every book I edit. I pore over every detail. I get anxious that I might have missed something crucial and have had many a sleepless night worrying about a grammatical point or an editorial decision I've made. I'm aware that this means I am often painstakingly slow, and I've lost contracts because I take so long. I can also totally lose it if some tiny detail isn't exactly how I want it. I wish I wasn't this perfectionist, but I can't help myself. One day I hope to write a novel myself, but I would probably never publish it or let anyone read it in case they didn't like it.

Monica, 58

I am extremely sensitive to any kind of criticism about my appearance or weight. If anyone tells me I look healthy, I immediately think that I must have put on weight. If anyone says I look tired, I instantly think I look old. I am very conscious of how I look and even well-meaning comments can send me into meltdown.

Gina, 38

Sensitive people tend to be perfectionists. Getting things wrong and failing is terrifying for them because they don't want to disappoint or let anyone down. If you were raised in a fiercely competitive home or school where anything but first place or winning was not valued, the drive towards perfectionism can become obsessive. But perfection is unattainable and is also rather dull, because if something is perfect it means there is no opportunity for growth. Perfectionists need to understand that there is nothing wrong with making mistakes as long as they learn and grow from them, and that crisis, disappointment and heartbreak can all be opportunities for personal growth.

Learn to see the value of making mistakes or getting things wrong. Sensitive people try so hard to be perfect, but perfection is static and dull. As long as you learn from your mistakes, you are evolving and growing. From a spiritual perspective, the purpose of our lives is to grow, and feeling out of your comfort zone is good because it is a sign you are challenging yourself and therefore evolving – but more about all that later in the book.

Compelled to solve others' problems

> Giving advice to others is something I feel absolutely
> compelled to do. If someone needs help, I can't refuse.
> It's who I am. I'll help people even without them asking
> me for that help, because, again, that's who I am. I live to
> and love to see others happy. It gives me a helper's high.
>
> Sonia, 44

Sensitive people often have an intense desire to help others or take responsibility for solving their problems. They go out of their way to be obliging and helpful. It's likely that this addiction to helping became ingrained during childhood, when their innate ability to sense the feelings of others meant they fell naturally and prematurely into the role of helper, fixer or carer. Indeed, many sensitive people take on the role of parent to their own parents and this gives them a maturity beyond their years.

Just because you feel someone else's pain does not mean you are responsible for it. Also, if you are always the one solving other people's problems or helping them, this prevents them from learning to become empowered by solving their own problems and helping themselves. It's not surprising that many sensitive parents are overprotective – smothering their children with their love. This is appropriate when a child simply can't fend for themselves, but it can become damaging when that child needs to spread their wings, learn from their mistakes and find their own way.

One of the hardest lessons for a sensitive person to learn is to stop gaining self-worth from feeling needed or by solving the issues of others. I'm one of life's fixers and helpers, and more often than not, my helping has backfired in the long-term, because I end up feeling resentful when there is no gratitude and my help is taken for granted and not acknowledged. If you discover the people you have done nothing but help and treat with respect have been exploiting you and betraying your trust behind your back, the pain is unbearable.

On the plus side, I have finally learned that I only need to help others when they actually ask for it, and to set boundaries to my helping. I also learned to release the compulsion I had to help others, because sometimes the best way to help others is to trust them to help themselves.

Soaking up everyone and everything

> I'm a teacher in a busy secondary school. Some of the children I teach come from very tough homes and every emotion gets thrown at me during the school day. I care deeply about my pupils and want nothing but the best for them. If I see a child crying because they can't cope with their work or they are having a tough time at home, I get upset too. I feel their anxiety. Every evening I have to spend at least half an hour just quietly processing my day and sorting out which emotion is mine and which doesn't belong to me. Sometimes I need far longer than that, and there are some days when I simply can't make it into school because my head and heart are in turmoil. My head teacher is concerned about the number of sick days I have taken.
>
> Sarah, 24

As mentioned in Chapter One, scientific studies show that sensitive people have heightened activity in specific areas of their brains and nervous systems than people who are less sensitive. This means that they have highly developed empathy, and not only sense other people's feelings but absorb and take them on as if they are their own. If you don't learn how to protect yourself against soaking up what isn't yours, this can lead to a loss of personal identity. Boundaries blur when you overidentify with other people and their feelings, and in time you may end up having absolutely no idea of who you are any more.

Hopefully by now you will be fully aware of your tendency to take on what isn't yours. If you aren't aware of this, it can become a seriously dangerous blind spot. You can end up feeling depressed and stressed for reasons that have nothing to do with you. In some cases, you may end up feeling physically unwell, as many sensitive people report actually feeling the pain of their loved ones when they are injured or sick.

You can also find your energy drained by soaking up the atmosphere or 'vibes' from an overstimulating, chaotic environment, such as an open-plan office, a crowded street or a shopping centre.

> Thank goodness for online shopping. I can't cope with the noise and pressure of shops. If I hear someone yelling across the street, cars honking their horns or loud music, it can actually hurt my ears. The last time I went to the high street was to buy a jacket. And I ended up buying one in a colour I hated because – and you won't believe this – I felt sorry for the shop assistant! She told me she was a colour therapist and she knew exactly what would suit me. She was such a kind lady and was so proud of her knowledge about the best colours for people to wear that I didn't have the heart to tell her I hated bright green or any bright colours because I don't like standing out. It's not just the pressure from shop assistants I find overwhelming when I shop, it's the uncertainty. At least if I buy online, I know I will be able to find what I am looking for.
>
> Seth, 20

> Sounds wrong, but social distancing during the pandemic felt easy for me. A relief.
>
> Mark, 31

If you are sensitive, you feel everything, from absorbing the emotions of others to crying at moving scenes in films (or even the adverts), and while this means you are super-empathetic and superb at connecting to others, it can also result in you feeling drained, stressed, tired or burnt out. Not being aware of this blind spot can make you feel depressed and unwell. You may spend a lot of time and money on unnecessary treatments and therapies which address the symptoms and not the cause.

What you may not realise is that your low moods and fatigue may be connected to sensory and emotional overload, and your pain may be empathetic or somehow absorbed from someone else. As you have the ability to process so much of what is going on around you, your sensitivity, rather than anything else, could be the cause. The answer is to learn how to manage your sensitivity, to set boundaries and to ensure you get the space and quiet time you need. In the next chapter I'll talk you through powerful strategies that can help you set those crucial boundaries.

The needs of others come first

> I simply can't be happy unless my loved ones and friends are happy and well cared for. The person who does that caring is usually me. I'm their rock and the place they can feel safe. To me, my feelings never seem as important as their feelings.
>
> Lara, 19

> I have this compulsion to help others, often at my own expense. I'm the one who pays the bills when others forget. I'm the one who never fails to remember birthdays, even for people I barely know. If there's a party, I'm the first to arrive and the last the leave, to help set things

up and to tidy them away. I'm the driver, the helper, the organiser. Nobody forces me into these roles, it's just who I am. It would be nice if people noticed and appreciated what I do more, but it's not something I'd ever point out.

Harry, 29

Due to your ability to feel the pain of others, you likely fell into the role of emotional caregiver from an early age and, over time, learned to subordinate your own emotions and place everyone else's happiness above your own. If you were brought up in a strictly religious household, you may also have been taught from an early age to be self-sacrificing, especially if you are female and gender stereotypes were enthusiastically reinforced.

You may not realise that overcaring for others can be just as damaging as neglecting them. When you do things for them that they should be doing for themselves, you are robbing them of their ability to step into their own power. A vital life lesson for sensitive people to learn is that, while the world is a better place when we all help each other, there is a fine line between helping others and controlling them.

In addition, if your focus is always on the needs of others and solving their problems, you aren't taking care of your own needs and solving your own problems, which, over time, can lead to chronic depression and low self-esteem. Sometimes you simply *have* to put yourself first – after all, once your own needs are met, you're in a stronger state to help others. This is why, in case of emergency on a plane, you are told to put on your own oxygen mask first before helping others, even your own children.

Millions of sensitive people are operating without enough oxygen, helping others when they themselves are wounded. What they need to see is that stepping into their own power and focusing more on their own needs will not only empower them but make them more effective helpers.

Do unto others

> I try to see the good in everyone and everything. When people treat me poorly or disrespect me, I am quick to forgive them and welcome them back. I want to give them another chance, as we all make mistakes. I have even ended up apologising when I'm not the one in the wrong, to restore communication and peace. I'm not perfect, so why should I expect others to be? I found out last year that my husband was cheating on me. It hurt like hell, but perhaps it was my fault because I have been so wrapped up in raising our children that maybe he felt neglected. He promised it didn't mean anything and I forgave him. But last week my friend told me my husband was still seeing his girlfriend. I don't believe her even though she says she has evidence. There must be some rational explanation, or it's a misunderstanding. He promised me he had left her.
>
> Sasha, 30

The belief that you should treat others as you wish to be treated yourself is a noble one. It is based on the ideal that there is good in everyone. Such beliefs may have a religious foundation or they may be what you were taught by your family or school. However, in the real world, they can be a recipe for disaster. You are likely to be taken advantage of and your trusting nature abused. Sometimes, however kind and considerate you are to others, you won't be appreciated in return. Sadly, there *isn't* goodness in everyone. Some people will always lie, cheat and have zero empathy, no matter how loving and forgiving you are.

Love is the most powerful force in the world, but it does not conquer all relationship problems. Unfortunately, people *don't* treat you as you treat them, they treat you *as you treat yourself.* The sad truth is that if you consistently place your own needs last and don't value yourself, then you can't expect others to consider your needs or value you either. But if you take small steps towards treating yourself well, you will soon notice that other people follow suit. More about all this in Chapter 4.

Move closer – but not too close

> People always want to get close to me and want me to get close to them too, but there are very few people whom I am truly close to. I love being around people and I give them my all when I am with them. However, I also need a lot of time out by myself, and many of my relationships fail because I need so much personal space.
>
> Philip, 45

You crave relationships and love people, but when they get too close you feel stifled. This can make you think there is something psychologically or emotionally damaged about you. However, as you'll see in in Chapter 4, where we discuss sensitive relationships in more depth, there is nothing wrong with you.

Sensitive souls have deep empathy for others and this means you feel what others are feeling. Unless you know how to manage this carefully, you can find interacting with other people confusing and draining. The answer is to surround yourself with people who understand and respect your need for space in relationships. Taking enough time to yourself when you are a sensitive person is as crucial as the air you breathe. Sometimes, this time out is difficult to achieve and tension mounts – for example, if you are raising a young family or working in a busy, chaotic environment. If this is the case, you need to find a middle way, because if you don't, the chances of your relationships or career thriving are minimal.

Conflict is bad

> They say childhood is the best time of your life, but it wasn't for me. I spent most nights with my head under my pillow, trying to drown out the sounds of my parents yelling at each other. On occasion, I heard them throwing and breaking things. Daytime was not much better. I spent most of my days walking on eggshells for fear of upsetting anyone and triggering another round of tension and arguments. Eventually, my parents got divorced, and in my early teens, I went to live with my mum. Things didn't get much better though, as she constantly dated guys who either drank too much or disrespected her in other ways. She never stood up to them and made it clear she didn't want me to either. My role was to be neither seen nor heard. I learned to avoid conflict, and to this day if anyone even raises their voice, I immediately want to leave the room. I can't stand up for myself or tell anyone how I really feel. I'm terrified of disagreements.
>
> Jasmine, 44

Somewhere along the line, the belief that conflict is bad became ingrained and you learned to repeatedly turn the other cheek, hide or run away to avoid it. This approach may have been a matter of survival when you were a vulnerable child and unable to assert yourself effectively to the adults in your life, but it is no longer viable when you become an adult yourself.

Perhaps when you were growing up you were consistently punished or criticised for speaking your mind or challenging the status quo. As a result, you learned not to believe in or express your own opinions, even though you are now an adult and perfectly entitled to have them.

Learning that you should not avoid conflict and that it is important to assert yourself, even if your opinion is not what others want to hear, are vital steps forward for sensitive souls.

Feelings are facts

> If I meet someone and I don't get a good feeling about them, I can't ignore it. Even when I am proved wrong and they turn out to be lovely, I keep my distance from them until my feelings tell me otherwise. It's the same with decisions I need to make in my life. I follow my feelings – always have, always will. I need to feel right before I commit to anyone or anything.
>
> Nia, 50

Sensitive souls feel their way through life. Their feelings are their compass and their guide.

Feelings can lift you up and pull you down. Sometimes these feelings are ones of joy, love and positivity, but they can also be fear, guilt, unworthiness, anger and other challenging emotions. When faced with negative feelings or by criticism or rejection from others, if you haven't learned how to manage or deal with your feelings, you might crumble or break down. Hurt feelings cut sensitive people deeper and for longer than other people.

Somewhere along the line – and this is particularly the case if you were born into an artistic or highly creative environment – you learned to place tremendous store on the power of your feelings and to minimise the value of logic and reason, or dismiss it as mundane. While the exclusively emotional approach to life has magic and merit, it also has many flaws.

If you have ever read Jane Austen's *Sense and Sensibility*, you will know what happens to Marianne Dashwood, the sister who is guided exclusively by her heart, in contrast to her more grounded sister, Elinor, who is guided by her head. While the reader admires Marianne's spontaneous and passionate approach to life, the inaccuracy of her powerful feelings almost kills her.

Part of becoming self-aware is learning to balance the demands of the heart with those of the head, and understanding that feelings are messengers of the truth but not truth itself.

Feelings are what make us feel alive but they are *not* facts.

Mind reading and fortune telling

> Whenever I receive an email from someone I know or work with, I pore over it. If the email is short and from a friend, and there is no affectionate signature or accompanying kiss, I'm convinced they are offended by something I have done. It's the same when I meet people. If they don't smile or give me a warm handshake, I immediately think they don't like me. In meetings, I scan the room and I feel like I know what everyone is thinking or going to say next, and I'm more often right than wrong in my assumptions.
>
> Jerry, 36

Sensitive people are often so convinced that they know what other people are thinking about them that they lose sight of the fact that while they could be right, they could also be wrong. There is no doubt they are highly intuitive, but they are also human. And humans can't accurately read minds or predict the future. Just because you believe you know what others are thinking about you, or what will happen next, doesn't make it reality. You can never know for sure what others are thinking or what is going to happen. Things may very well turn out the way you anticipate, but they may also turn out completely differently.

And it's not just what you believe others are thinking that could be wrong. What you are thinking about yourself could also be wrong. Just as feelings happen to you but do not define you, you are not simply what you think. And thinking something does *not* make it true. Learn to use your intuition as a guide, but always consider the factual evidence, too.

I'm crazy

It was my daughter's wedding day. When the service began and she walked beside me towards her husband-to-be, my mind was crowded with fond memories of her childhood. She's my only daughter and I felt every single memory. When we finally reached the altar, my face was wet with tears. I also had no idea where I was. I was lost for a few moments. I turned around to see everyone in the church staring at me. There were a few nervous coughs too, as my daughter was trying to disengage from my arm but I was frozen. We had rehearsed the ceremony twice before, but I suddenly couldn't remember a thing. The vicar then asked me to hand my daughter over to the groom. In my head I heard myself reading bedtime stories to my daughter. It was crazy!

Eventually my wife came up to me, gently untangled me from my daughter and guided me to my seat. I was really out of it. I felt terrible for holding things up on my daughter's special day. Everything had been planned and rehearsed and I was the one causing delays. I had this overwhelming urge to run away, and that's exactly what I then did. The service started without me and although I did return halfway through, after I'd pulled myself together, I'll always regret not being there for all of it.

Sean, 57

When life gets overwhelming, either emotionally or because of external stimuli, people who are not aware of their sensitive natures can have difficulty thinking. They may even shut down or feel as if they are going insane – and behave as if they are, too. They may suddenly be struck by an urge they can't understand to abruptly and inappropriately leave the situation. In fact, they aren't going insane, they are just suffering from sensory overload and this is entirely normal for them.

It's my fault

> When I'm driving and I hear someone hooting a horn, I'm immediately convinced they are hooting at me, even if I have done nothing wrong. Likewise, when I hear a police siren, I get this overwhelming feeling of guilt. There must be something wrong with my car or perhaps my driving. When people are distant towards me, I always think it must be something I have done. Whenever things don't go as planned, somehow I think it must be my fault.
>
> Sajid, 45

Humankind is always trying to explain why things happen. When things don't work out as planned, we look for someone or something to blame. Many people look to blame others, certain circumstances or even the weather! People who are sensitive or feeling sensitive tend to immediately blame themselves and take responsibility when things go wrong.

You should have known better. You weren't good enough. Your instinctive response is to take responsibility for everything and everyone.

One of the ways you try to ensure that things don't go wrong is to meticulously plan and over-control. Although this approach can be highly successful, it doesn't allow for or prepare you for the unexpected. And if you apply this approach to relationships, you can make the other person feel stifled.

It's impossible for anyone to be in control of every factor that might create a problem, but it's not easy for sensitive people to let go and take a more philosophical approach. By not blaming yourself, you will be in a better mindset to tackle the problem and find something positive to take from the situation.

Overthinking

> Any purchase I make, I consider very carefully. Even if I find something that is absolutely perfect and within my price range, I have to see what else is out there. Once I have finally considered as many options as possible and have returned to purchase what I originally decided on, I will continue to explore the other options I could have bought but didn't. It can get exhausting at times.
>
> Rachel, 24

Sensitive people are constantly on high alert. They think about everything and everyone at the same time. It can take them forever to make even simple decisions, such as which sandwich to have for lunch. Then, when they finally decide, they are likely to continue weighing the alternatives afterwards and second-guess themselves.

In matters both major and trivial, they carefully consider every possible scenario. Given this tendency to overanalyse, it's not surprising that many sensitive people suffer from insomnia and anxiety. They have a hard time letting go of possibilities, by day and by night.

Because of their relentless overthinking, sensitive people can blow inconsequential things, which others might consider trivial, out of all proportion. For example, someone innocently looking the other way is a perceived slight, or someone ignoring your text means you have offended them. You endlessly pore over everything that happens, typically against a worst-case-scenario backdrop. And despite your ability to see the bigger picture, you've lost sleep and peace of mind for no reason. I suffer from this particular blind spot myself. In the introduction, I told the story of my interview on *Under the Skin*, and how for five long months afterwards I imagined it was a disaster – to the point where my unnecessary fretting made me feel unwell. I've learned from this experience to try not to overthink or revisit things, because more often than not the worrying is entirely unnecessary.

Indeed, I have also learned that all worrying is futile. Worrying about something does not change it or achieve anything. We tend to think we are actually doing something when we worry, but we aren't doing anything. We are just wasting our energy! If something is concerning you, take positive action, and if nothing positive can be done then accept that and let go.

Or, in the words of the Serenity Prayer author Reinhold Niebuhr, 'Have the courage to change the thing I can and the serenity to accept the things I cannot change. And the wisdom to know the difference.'

People-pleasing

> It seems like I've been saying 'sorry' or 'let's do things your way' or 'I don't want to bother you' or 'it's only me' for my entire life. I can't help it, but I feel that other people are always busier, more important or better than I am in some way and I can't possibly inconvenience them. I make a point of ensuring I am not bothering anyone. Another thing I find myself saying a lot is 'no problem', but it *is* a problem, because I find myself running around after everyone and it's getting exhausting.
>
> Lucy, 33

> The worst thing for me is to feel that I have offended someone. I worry endlessly about hurting people's feelings. I want to make other people happy, so, for example, if someone wants to go out to a restaurant and asks what I would like to eat, I tell them I'll like whatever they decide. I find it super hard to say no. I'm the person who is there whenever my friends want me to be there for them. I will listen for hours, neglecting to do what I need to do.
>
> Anna, 40

Sensitive people carefully consider the feelings of others. They want to make other people feel welcome and special, but this 'don't mind me' approach can seriously backfire. In your desire to create harmony you may end up saying yes when you mean no, no when you mean yes and pretending to be someone you are not.

This desire to please people may have become a habit when you were a child and instructed to do as you were told or to agree with people who were in authority, but as with so many things from childhood, when you enter adulthood it is time to put this away. You need to learn that no matter how hard you try, you will never make everyone happy. There are always going to be people who agree with you and people who disagree with you, and another group of people who are undecided or indifferent. Always be yourself, because how other people respond to you is their choice, not yours.

Odd one out

> Things that other people enjoy or say are cool either bore me or leave me feeling overwhelmed. In my student years I loathed alcohol and big parties. I thought there was something wrong with me. If only I had known that I was highly sensitive and more suited to intimate gatherings.
>
> Shelley, 42

It took me far too long to learn how to deal with small talk. I can't stand it. It takes so much emotional energy for me to talk to people on a superficial level. I am good at listening and paying attention, but talking to someone I don't know about their holidays or their kitchen extension or the weather is torture. I much prefer to have one-to-one conversations with people I know. That's why parties in general are not a natural fit for me. I'm always weighing up in my mind when would be the optimum and polite time for me to make my excuses and leave.

Linda, 29

Feeling as if you don't belong, that there is something wrong with you or you are the odd one out or, in some extreme cases, that you are from a different planet, likely began in childhood. Your sensitive approach to life set you apart from your family and peers, so you learned to mask or hide it, to try to 'fit in', so as not to draw attention to yourself.

Fitting in socially is incredibly important during childhood, but later in life you really don't need to continue to operate in this way. You need to learn the importance of protecting your empathetic energy from other people, because if you don't, you risk losing yourself and the ability to set boundaries. This is especially important in professional or work settings where you can't bring emotion into everything and sometimes need to make tough decisions. For you, overthinking and over-feeling is entirely normal and part of who you are. You need to step back from people-pleasing and respect your need to withdraw regularly to a place of peace and calm to avoid system overload.

Uncomfortable with praise, observation and attention

I had this nightmare boss. He had this habit of standing over me while I worked. What he didn't understand was that the closer he watched over me, the poorer my performance. In the end I complained to human resources about it because it was making me feel ill. I'm the same if I know someone is waiting for me to finish something. I can't concentrate. All I can think about is them waiting for me. So, if someone says 'take your time' to me, they need to understand that as long as they are watching or waiting, it won't get done. I can't focus at all.

John, 30

You may long to be noticed or praised, but then when you finally receive attention you may feel extremely uncomfortable. Sensitive people have a habit of apologising a lot or shying away from the spotlight. (How many times have you said 'it's only me'?) They also tend to underplay their accomplishments so as not to make others feel inferior or less than. In short, they diminish themselves to make others feel better.

This urge to hide or diminish their own power is perhaps one of their most damaging blind spots. It goes right to the heart of the matter. Sometimes it is not other people or situations that disempower sensitives, it is themselves. You become your own worst enemy. I can think of no better place to defer to one of the most inspiring poems ever written. It is by a famous spiritual author called Marianne Williamson, who recently presented the case for sensitives to stand in their own power on the global stage. She made a passionate plea for the forces of love and kindness to counter hate and darkness during her campaign to become the Democratic candidate for President of the United States. If you have never read her words before, read them slowly now and let the profound wisdom into your heart and mind. You may also want to share them with any sensitive person you know. This is a short extract, and I encourage you to seek out the full version yourself. [18]

18 Williamson, M. (1992) *A Return to Love: Reflections on the Principles of A Course in Miracles*. HarperCollins. p.190.

There's nothing enlightened about shrinking
So that other people do not feel insecure around you.
We are all meant to shine […]
And as we let our own light shine,
We unconsciously give other people permission to do
the same.

Your aversion to praise and attention may be related to something or someone in your life humiliating you, or to feelings of low self-esteem due to lack of understanding about your sensitive nature. Whatever the case, it's crucial for your well-being that you work on valuing yourself as much as you value other people. It's vital to understand that when you value yourself, you inspire others to do the same. As the poem says, there is nothing positive about diminishing yourself so others do not feel insecure. This doesn't mean becoming boastful or arrogant, it just means taking humble pride in who you are and what you are achieving with your life.

Closely linked to this innate aversion to praise and attention is an intense dislike of being observed. If other people are watching your performance in any way, this can disorientate you, and it's one reason why sensitive people don't tend to thrive in environments where their time is tightly structured or controlled by other people and their performance constantly monitored. They need their freedom. Knowing this about yourself, avoid situations where you will be watched or monitored if you can. If you do find yourself being observed, practising the art of detachment (see Chapter 3) will help you to cope.

One technique that has always helped me is a strategy that should come very naturally to sensitives – I think less about how I appear and more about how I can help or benefit the person watching me. That takes the focus away from needing praise or validation from others, or thinking about how you appear to them, and places it firmly on what others can gain from you.

And if that doesn't work, you can always try the Winston Churchill method, which is to imagine your audience naked!

Truth-seekers

> I want to help people so much it is hard for me to see when I am being taken advantage of. If I'm stopped in the street by a salesperson, my heart goes out to them and I end up signing up for something I don't really want. I'm gullible, I guess. I have this habit of believing everything people say. It doesn't enter my mind that people won't have my best interests at heart.
>
> Mike, 27

Sensitive people make terrible liars. The only time they can say something they don't mean is when they hope it will help or make someone else feel better. Never ask them if they like your new haircut, because they will say yes even if it's a disaster. But apart from those kinds of white lies, they are often people of great integrity. The problem is they think that everyone else has the same relationship with truth as them, which can make them extremely gullible. Finding it so hard to lie themselves, when they do come across someone who is an accomplished liar, they are very easily taken in. They can quite literally believe anything they are told.

As mentioned previously many times, in my personal and professional life, I have trusted people completely, only to find out that they have been taking advantage of me or were using me for self-serving reasons. Each time I tell myself I will never be so gullible again, but then it happens again. I pride myself on being good at reading people, but when it comes to people who are fake or seasoned liars, I'm like a lamb to the slaughter.

If you recognise yourself in any of this, you need to understand that sadly not everyone tells the truth.

Be nice

> People tell me I am like Pollyanna – that girl who always saw the best in everyone and everything. I like to be thought of as sunny and optimistic – a nice, cheerful person. If people are rude or I am treated unfairly, I stay upbeat and don't tell them how I feel. I can't be unkind. Sometimes, though, I need to hide away and punch pillows really hard. I never let anyone see. My anger is perfectly hidden, and so it should be, because I don't like feeling that way. It's ugly and I want life to be beautiful.
>
> Ariel, 19

Kind-hearted, gentle people typically struggle to deal with any negative emotions, such as anger and jealousy. Their instinctive response is to repress anything that feels unkind or 'not nice'. They find themselves being nice by default whenever they encounter negativity, either from others or within themselves. Rather than face negative emotions within themselves, they refuse to acknowledge they exist.

However, emotions happen for a reason. It is important to acknowledge your negative emotions, and the lessons they have to teach you. If you don't, they become hidden and express themselves as low self-esteem, depression and poor health. By acknowledging and facing your negative emotions, you also help to release them and move on.

Time to refocus

Now you've read the most common blind spots for sensitive souls, remember not to fall into the trap of thinking that blind spots are all negative or signs of weaknesses, defects or flaws in your personality. When something is in the shadows it simply means it is hidden and the light of your conscious awareness hasn't shone on its potential.

Let's refocus and now turn the bright spotlight of your conscious awareness onto some of the remarkable positive personality traits of being sensitive. You may find that you don't immediately identify these as remarkable, because they come naturally and feel totally everyday to you. Or perhaps previous attempts to understand yourself better have focused on what is challenging about your personality rather than what is good. Sadly, sensitive people are quick to recognise their flaws, slow to recognise their blind spots and even slower to acknowledge their gifts.

If you have found reading this chapter challenging, let what follows bring you a welcome dose of comfort, and be reminded yet again that sensitivity is *not* a weakness but a strength – a very real blessing. It's time for you to acknowledge and honour your positive traits.

Count your blessings

Thanks to your sensitivity, you have truly beautiful blessings to share with the world. Like everything in life, sometimes there are downsides, but you can learn to manage those, and it's not a heavy price to pay for the incredible upsides. So, what are these upsides? In no particular order, I've counted them out for you below. As a sensitive, you are:

1. Empathetic
2. Intuitive

3. Imaginative and creative
4. Compassionate
5. Drawn to nature
6. In tune with animals
7. Concerned for the well-being of others and the good of the team
8. Kind
9. Polite and respectful
10 Appreciative
11. Honest
12. Generous
13. Observant
14. A potential healer
15. Able to see the bigger picture or behind the curtain to what is really going on
16 Able to see or sense what others don't
17. Loyal
18. A deep and curious thinker
19. Possessed of a rich inner world
20. Dedicated
21. Able to solve problems
22. Attentive to sensory details in environments
23. Alert to subtle nuances in social interactions
24. A potential psychic
25. Spiritually insightful and wise

In my opinion, among the most transformative gifts of being sensitive are empathy and intuition. Indeed, these qualities have such extraordinary potential for sensitive people to heal themselves and others that I can't do them justice here, so I decided to devote Chapter 6 in this book to them.

Another remarkable gift is the ability to see magic – or what is extraordinary in the ordinary. Sensitive souls notice the sensory or tiny details others miss and can find great contentment in the little things, such as a smile, a well-made bed or a tidy sock drawer. They notice subtle colours, fragrances, sounds and other rich details intensely. They especially appreciate it when people do things they don't have to, such as holding open doors or going over and above the call of duty – for example, a barista who takes a little extra time to make sure the chocolate sprinkles on your cappuccino form a perfect heart shape; or when someone politely ignores a text they receive while they are talking to you.

Sensitive people are also those to whom others instinctively turn during times of crisis or when they need to be heard. Many Samaritans and crisis call centres are staffed by sensitive souls with remarkable abilities to listen with empathy. Given that many sensitive people have struggled themselves, they can offer great understanding and acceptance to others. Other people feel heard, understood and 'seen' by them, because they listen without judgement. Talking to a sensitive person feels like a safe place to express feelings, and as a result they are often sought out for their wisdom and guidance. They rarely make hasty decisions and carefully consider the options.

Perhaps most wonderful of all, and a gift they seldom realise or take credit for, is the ability of a sensitive person to make others feel welcome and at home. It is incredibly reassuring – comforting, even – to be in their company, and when they are not around, the feeling of security they bring is sorely missed.

> I would not describe myself as a sensitive person. I'm pragmatic and have a black-and-white approach to life, but I have learned to truly value having people in your life who are on the sensitive side. To give an example, I'm a barrister and my legal assistant, Penny, is a sensitive soul. She takes her work very seriously and can get overemotional when things don't go our way or

when heavy demands are placed on her by me and my team. At first, it used to frustrate me because she is so talented and it seemed that her sensitivity to any kind of criticism, oversight or setback was holding her back. Then, she went on maternity leave for a year and was replaced by someone who was just as talented but didn't invest themselves in their work as much as she did. I can't describe it, but the place felt cold and lifeless without her. She was sorely missed. I'm very glad she is back now and so is the rest of our team.

Laura, 54

When you review the list of blessings above, it makes sense that sensitive souls are often drawn to artistic, creative, caring and healing professions as well as to careers, such as law, that involve research, acute observation and meticulous attention to detail. It's also no surprise that many sensitive people are managers, therapists and teachers, or committed to charity work, protecting the environment or animal welfare. However, sensitive people can be found in all kinds of careers and businesses, and the world is a better and more colourful place for it, because they act as a peace and harmony loving counterbalance to the prevalence of narcissism and materialism.

Out of sync

'Life isn't fair' is a mantra you have probably heard many times. You just have to accept and deal with that. But if you are sensitive, you likely can't accept that injustice and cruelty are here to stay and that's just the way things are. You see the potential for a better world and want to make a difference. However, if you live in a culture that doesn't place great value on gentleness, you may feel out of sync or too sensitive for the world you live in.

Certain cultures are more receptive to sensitivity than others. In China, for example, there is emphasis on the importance of politeness and respect. In Italy and Spain, acts of kindness towards strangers are routinely celebrated. Scandinavian countries are regarded as home to the world's happiest people because of their cultural emphasis on the well-being of the collective rather than the individual, as well as their deep connection to nature. In Japan, an awareness of nuance is considered essential for success and happiness, and forest bathing to escape the demands of daily life is even recommended by the government. It's similar in Thailand where the people are known to be 'gentle' and where indirect communication that is unlikely to offend or upset is preferred. 'Indirect' communication is valued.

Sadly, there is a long way to go in materialistic societies like ours, but the more we start celebrating our sensitive souls rather than dismissing them as liabilities or flaws, the more this will change. It is possible to thrive as a sensitive person in a culture that isn't as sensitive as it could be, but you need to manage your sensitivity, accept you are going to have to go against the tide, ensure you avoid getting overwhelmed and focus on your strengths.

I can't repeat this enough: if you have ever thought that your sensitive soul weakens you, makes you less of a good person or is a flaw, it is truly time for you to understand that there is huge strength in your gentleness.

From now on, whenever you feel the urge to 'fit in', the desire to be more like other people or to respond from your blind spots rather than conscious awareness, count your blessings instead. Use them as your guide. This not only empowers you but also empowers others, because listening to, caring for, helping and healing others and seeing the magic in the everyday is what a sensitive person is born to do. It's also what we need to make the world a more beautiful place.

Your natural empathy, intuition, kindness, generosity, compassion and creativity are beautiful qualities that the world needs far more of, not far less. You embody those qualities or have the potential to embody them whenever you feel sensitive. Within you is the power to reveal their value and their strength to others. Many problems associated with sensitivity occur when you hide or repress your instincts. Please, please don't try to hide who you are any more. Every time you hide, condemn or dismiss gentleness as a liability, you do not only do yourself but the world a great disservice.

More to come

Many sensitive people have absolutely no idea how highly regarded they often are. People who care do stand out, just not in the obvious ways. Yes, other people will rarely tell them how much they value them, and others will frequently take advantage of their good natures. But you can learn to strike a healthy balance between giving and taking. Others recognise the power of your special qualities but the person who needs to recognise them now is you. Once you recognise and value your specialness you truly can become an unstoppable force.

The knowledge

In the previous chapter, I mentioned my time working in an old people's home. When patients were close to passing away, I would sometimes get the opportunity to speak to them about their lives. Many were lonely and very keen to talk and share. Without exception they spoke about what they had *felt* and *given* in their lives, rather than what they had done and taken. Many of them, sensitive by nature or not, regretted not having had the courage to believe in their hearts more. Many of them regretted not understanding what really mattered in life sooner. None of them regretted any of the times they felt sensitive.

Decades later, when people started to send me their stories about death and dying for my spiritual books, a similar theme occurred. The biggest regret of those close to death was not understanding themselves better and leaving it too late to value the importance of sensitive traits such as empathy, kindness, intuition and, of course, love. Now that you have greater understanding of your own innate sensitive traits, you don't need an awareness of your mortality to awaken you to the beauty, blessings and raw power of your sensitivity. You have self-knowledge now. It is your gentle power. Find the courage to know yourself and to value who you truly are. Don't hide your light.

Given that you have a remarkable ability to understand others, feel deeply and to process so clearly what is going on around you, you owe it to yourself to be just as aware of what is happening *within* you, too. You may not be able to sense all your blind spots and blessings right away, as learning about yourself is a lifelong journey and not all of those mentioned here will necessarily apply to you. Give yourself all the time you need to get to know yourself better, and please don't avoid acknowledging and working through your blind spots. You will never progress by staying in your comfort zone. Sure, it is challenging to acknowledge your sensitivity and all that implies, but every time you face rather than avoid challenges in your life, you evolve.

Armed with greater self-knowledge and insight into your personality – both your blinds spots and your blessings – it's time to unleash the secret power of your gentleness. Pause for a moment. Take a long, deep breath in. Then exhale completely. As you slowly expel all the air in your lungs, imagine you are letting go of the past and all those times you tried to 'fit in'. Pause for another moment. Then inhale sharply and turn the page. You are now ready to unlock the sensitivity code itself.

Coming up...

The next chapter, Unlocking the Sensitivity Code, will offer proven tools and strategies you can immediately use. Apply them to your life, and wherever you are on the sensitivity spectrum, they will help you grow in self-acceptance, enable you to deal with the challenges sensitive people regularly encounter and boost your self-esteem. Unlocking the Sensitivity Code is a healing journey from the inside out. I hope the suggestions offered will empower you not only to survive but to thrive. Fasten your seat belt – it's going to be a breathtaking, life-changing ride.

CHAPTER 3

Unlocking the Sensitivity Code

Hopefully what you have read so far has encouraged you to become aware of who you are and what gentle aspects of yourself you may have suppressed, denied or hidden because you felt they were weak or unacceptable. I hope you will also be experiencing some stirrings of excitement about your potential. Carry that growing self-awareness and excitement forward into this chapter, as you learn how to unlock the very real power of your sensitivity.

If you struggle to cope with the challenges of being or feeling sensitive, the chances are you are approaching your life in a way that isn't allowing you to develop and showcase your full potential. It's like not having the correct PIN to unlock and use the amazing functions of your smartphone. This chapter presents 12 strategies to help you unlock the potential of your sensitivity code and transform the challenges of being a gentle person into a strength. They are based on strategies proven to be effective by scientists and psychologists, my own years of research, what works for me and what sensitive people consistently tell me empowers them.

Take three weeks

Before you begin, I need you to set aside at least three weeks. Rome wasn't built in a day, and unlocking your sensitivity code can't happen in a day either. You need at least 21 days, which is the absolute minimum amount of time that research tells us is required for new patterns of thought and behaviour to imprint themselves on the brain and become a catalyst for positive change.[19]

Make a promise to yourself that for the next three weeks you will follow these 12 sensitivity solutions. Take these small but powerful steps every single day. Don't think initially in terms of the rest of your life, because your conscious mind will rebel before you even start to experience the benefits. Allow yourself to make a choice to continue when the three weeks of incorporating these strategies in your life are over. Let the solutions prove to you that their benefits are real and it is in your best interests to keep going for the rest of your life.

You may want to focus on incorporating one solution at a time, fully integrating it into your life before assimilating the next one. But bear in mind that the 12 unlocking codes are complementary to each other. They work best in synergy and are at their most transformative when applied as a combination.

And one more vital thing before you begin: don't let all this life-changing information remain in the world of thought or theory. The perception shift here is designed to encourage you to *take action* in your daily life. Don't read the knowledge, think about it and keep on going about your life in exactly the same way. Sensitive people are prone to overthinking and indecision. There is undoubted power in your thoughts, but research shows there may be even greater power in your actions.[20] If you've ever learned that the only way to trust a person is by their actions and not their words, you will know the truth of this. It is not what you *think* but what you *do* that matters. To paraphrase the ancient but always profound wisdom of Aristotle, 'You are what you repeatedly *do*.'

So take that first step now – you won't regret it!

19 Lally, P. *et al.* (2010) 'How are habits formed: Modelling habit formation in the real world.' *Journal of European Psychology*, 40(6), 998–1009.

20 Neal, D. *et al.* (2013) 'How do people adhere to goals when will power is low? The profits and pitfalls of strong habits.' *American Journal of Personality and Social Psychology*, 104(6) 959–75.

Sensitivity Code 1: Look within

If you often feel that you don't fit in or that there is something wrong or defective about you, if you worry that people will reject you for revealing your true feelings, if you often feel lonely in a crowded room or that you are too sensitive for this world, the chances are you have spent your life seeking validation externally rather than by looking deep within. You have likely looked to other people to give you a sense of belonging, to your work or career for a sense of meaning, to material things to make you feel safe.

Whenever you seek validation outside yourself, you are like a reed blowing in the wind, because external factors are outside your control. The only way to find true and lasting peace and joy, and the answers you are seeking, is to find them from the *inside out*. Happiness isn't the result of achieving material goals but of finding inner peace. The problem is, many sensitive people are incredibly fearful of looking within themselves for answers because of the feelings of isolation and confusion they may encounter there.

The previous chapter began the essential work by helping you become more aware of your inner landscape and how it shapes your life. The more conscious you become of your blind spots, the more you will see how inaccurate perceptions and responses have been dictating the direction of your life. As I have repeatedly stressed, self-knowledge does not happen overnight. It is a constant work in progress, but nothing in your life will change for the better until you start to look within.

Once you increase your self-knowledge, you will find that it becomes so much easier to identify the direction you want your life to head in, what has been dragging you down and what you need to let go of. You will also find that those things that you thought mattered so greatly don't bring you the fulfilment they seemed to promise. You will see them as futile attempts to avoid facing the loneliness and emptiness within.

Letting go of things, people and coping patterns that prevent you from being the best version of yourself can be an extreme challenge. Sensitive people are often nostalgic and loyal, and saying goodbye to anyone or anything is traumatic for them. It can also trigger intense fears of isolation and making the wrong decision, and send them right back to toxic relationships or unhealthy coping behaviours. However, until you are willing to acknowledge and face your inner fears, the door to personal growth and fulfilment in your life will remain firmly locked.

Unlock and take action

Research has shown that an effective way to dissolve fear is to face it – but to face it gradually and repeatedly.[21] Whenever you feel anxious, this simple but highly effective mini-meditation will set things in motion gently, if practised on a daily basis.

Take a few minutes each day to sit alone in total silence. Switch off your phone, make sure you won't be disturbed, close your eyes and just focus on your breathing. Notice any thoughts and emotions that surface, but don't engage with them. Simply observe them. Just because you think or feel something does not mean it's true. Instead of being intimidated by any feelings of anxiety and fear, ask them what they are trying to tell or teach you. Reframe your anxiety as your teacher, a source of wisdom. When you feel ready, open your eyes and take a big stretch. Repeat the meditation as often as is needed or whenever you feel anxious.

Your aim here is to get you more accustomed to searching for answers from within rather than seeking them externally and to feel peace rather than feelings of emptiness whenever you are alone with yourself.

21 Frankland, P.W. *et al.* (2018) 'Facing your fears.' *Science*, 360(6394), 1186–1187.

Sensitivity Code 2: Grow up again

Childhood is the place where we learn lessons about love and what truly matters in life, and these lessons can last a lifetime. When unconditional love isn't freely given by your parents and carers, you learn that love is conditional on what you do for others, rather than on who you are. Likewise, if you have been neglected by parents and carers, the lesson you learn is that you and your needs don't matter.

If you grew up receiving conditional love, it is not surprising that you instinctively take on the role of people-pleaser in all your adult relationships, hoping to receive the love or acceptance you never got as a child. If you grew up being neglected, or worse still, abused, it is hardly surprising that you suffer from low self-esteem. And if you grew up being bullied or criticised because of your sensitive soul, it is no surprise you try to repress or hide your sensitivity and regard it as a weakness.

No childhood is ever perfect and not all sensitive people have traumatic childhoods, but many do feel the need in their adult life to pretend to be someone they are not. More often than not the role they fall into is one of people-pleaser, but other inauthentic roles they adopt include the giver, the helper, the eternal optimist, the high achiever buried in their work, the person who provides for everyone but themselves, or the victim or addict drowning out their pain by abusing themselves.

To reconnect with your authentic self and release the need to pretend to be someone you are not, you need to acknowledge the damage done to the heart and mind of your inner child. Once you hear that pain, you can set yourself free from the need to pretend to be someone you are not, and give yourself the unconditional love, compassion, kindness and support that your inner child never had. By parenting yourself in this way you give yourself the chance to grow up again, but this time believing in yourself, without needing other people or things to validate you.

Unlock and take action

The only person who can heal the wounds of your inner child is you. Reconnecting with your inner child to heal yourself rather than looking to others to make you feel whole sounds easy in theory, but I know – and many other sensitive people with a wounded inner child also know – that in practice it is not. Sometimes it can be hard to know where to begin. This visualisation technique is a great starting point.

> You need some peace and quiet and at least ten minutes for this visualisation. Find a photograph of yourself as a child. If you don't have one, instead recall a memorable image of yourself as a child. Look at that photograph or see your childhood image in your mind's eye and visualise meeting that younger version of yourself. Allow your adult self to tell that child that they are unique, valued and loved for who they are. There is no need to prove themselves to anyone and nothing to be ashamed or feel guilty about. Tell them you are proud of them and that from now on, whenever they feel scared, rejected, alone or in need of validation, you will instantly be there. Tell them they are going to be okay. Apologise for not having been there in the past whenever they felt in pain, or for pushing them to impress others. Tell them you will not allow anyone who is not respectful of them into their world. Reassure them that whenever they feel sensitive or emotional, you will be there to speak up for them and support them. When you are ready to finish your visualisation, imagine that you are placing your inner child in your heart. Tell them that this is their true home from now on, where they will always be safe and protected. You will always be there for them.

In your daily life, every time you feel anxious or that you have to wear a mask and pretend, visualise your inner child and how they would be feeling. Don't allow any more pain to be inflicted on that inner child. Don't let old wounds reopen. Carry your conscious awareness of your inner child, growing up again in your heart, with you in all areas of your life. Do things that will make your inner child feel safe and happy. Make a big fuss of any achievement as well as on their birthday and special days. Allow them to be creative and authentic. Allow them to trust themselves, because they know you will not allow anything inauthentic into their life ever again because 'they' are 'you'.

Sensitivity Code 3: Love being different

Sensitive souls often think they are weak, or too different from everyone else to ever really belong or be accepted. Because they tend to see the world through the eyes of other people, they experience low self-esteem and loss of personal identity. They spend their lives trying not to be seen as different. Although they are often the first people others turn to in times of crisis, they struggle to see their own value. Indeed, many sensitives suffer from what psychologists describe as 'imposter syndrome'. This syndrome describes feeling that you are not the person others think you are and that any success is undeserved or not of your own making. You feel like an imposter in your own life.

To step into your own power, as a sensitive, you need to remind yourself on a daily basis that there is absolutely nothing wrong with being different. Being different does not mean being broken. Being different is *good*.

Unlock and take action

The best way to make an impression on others is to be yourself. But old habits die hard for sensitives, and if you have got into a habit of doubting yourself, thinking you aren't good enough or don't belong, or that there is something wrong with you, what should you do when imposter syndrome strikes yet again or you feel the need to blend in? Simple. You focus less on what is negative and more on what is positive about feeling uncomfortable or different.

Consider how your life would be if you never felt uncomfortable or different again. Imagine yourself effortlessly fitting in everywhere. Chances are you would be a 'nice' but very dull person who wasn't going to push the boundaries or achieve much in their life.

Research on imposter syndrome has indicated that it is most common among high achievers and successful creatives.[22] It is often what drives such people to achieve their success, because it is at its most powerful when they are pushing themselves or doing something new or challenging. Imposter syndrome doesn't ever strike when you are operating in your comfort zone because your comfort zone is not the place where personal growth happens. So when imposter syndrome or self-doubt strike, it is healthy, because it suggests you are in a situation that is potentially going to challenge you and therefore help you grow as a person.

From now on, consciously make an effort to shift your focus away from the negatives about feeling different and focus on the positives instead. You feel uncomfortable or like an outsider because you need to step out of your comfort zone and evolve in the process. Switch feelings of anxiety to feelings of excitement. Your authentic self is calling out to you to reclaim it.

Love being different. Stop comparing yourself negatively to others. Every time you do that, the message you send yourself and the universe is that you are not worthy or good enough. *The Sensitivity Code* is all about discovering that you are enough. Other people and external things can't ever complete you, despite what the movies and advertising would have you believe. You are

22 www.apa.org/gradpsych/2013/11/fraud

worthy. The only person you need to impress and the only person who can complete you is YOU.

Accept who you are and remind yourself that true power, beauty and success are found *within*. If you are a gentle and kind person or you are feeling sensitive, you can't be anything other than who you are. Celebrate your sensitivity. Say this affirmation out loud or with your thoughts every morning on waking and every evening before sleep: *I am exactly who I am meant to be. I am enough. I am whole and strong. I belong. What I reveal is needed in this world.*

The reason you need to affirm it to yourself on waking and before sleep is because these are the two times in your day when your mind is most receptive to new perspectives. You are between sleeping and waking at these times. Your brainwaves are in theta.

Delta is the state your brain is in when you are unconscious or fast asleep. Theta is when you are in a state of deep relaxation on waking or falling asleep. Alpha is when you are awake, calm and becoming more alert, beta when you are fully awake, active and busy and gamma when you are fully concentrated and alert.

The theta state is where the brains of young children settle[23]. As adults we tend to unconsciously revert to what was programmed into us when we were under the age of seven, even if our more mature minds think otherwise. In essence, theta brainwaves are the optimum state for reprogramming your mind. When you are fully awake and your brain becomes more active in alpha, beta or gamma, your brain is not as receptive to reprogramming.

Your brain also responds to repetition. Do these morning and evening affirmations for at least three weeks – the minimum amount of time psychologists believe it takes to reprogramme your mind and replace negative beliefs and behaviours with more positive ones. During the day, reinforce them as often as

23 Fattinger, S. *et al.* (2017) 'Theta waves in children's waking electroencephalogram resemble local aspects of sleep during wakefulness.' *Scientific Reports*, 7, 1118.

you can. Write down 'I am complete' on a sticky note and post it on your fridge, mirror or computer. You could also incorporate hack-proof variations of 'I am complete' or something similar in your passwords, so you have to constantly type it out. The more your brain sees, reads and hears this positive messaging, the more likely you are to believe it and behave accordingly.

Sensitivity Code 4: Reach for the stars

If you've been applying the first three sensitivity solutions to your life, you may now be beginning to experience inner shifts. When you start to change on the inside, this will impact what is going on in your life on the outside. However, at this early stage you may find that instead of feeling empowered you feel even more vulnerable than before.

If this is the case, it is more important than ever that you keep unlocking your sensitivity code. You are undergoing a transformation, and change is always going to be unsettling. Keep going. You are experiencing the darkness before the dawn, the labour pains before the birth, perhaps even the 'dark night of the soul' that precedes every remarkable transformation.

Every person's experience is different, and some people experience a darker transformation than others, but however you are experiencing it, rest assured that feeling conflicted and insecure at this point is where you need to be. It's a sign that you are growing, and sometimes you may get growing pains. If you are tempted to run away, imagine how abandoned your inner child would feel. Find within yourself the courage to protect and stay with that child.

Unlock and take action

It takes real courage to face your fears and reconnect with your authentic self. If you find yourself feeling anxious and tempted to revert back to feeling 'less than', try this simple but surprisingly effective technique.

> Stand up, pull your shoulders back and place your hands on your hips. Strike a superhero pose. Then, put your feet apart and stretch as high and as wide as you can, while opening your mouth and yawning as loudly as you can. (If you want to roar, feel free.) In those blissful moments as you reach for the stars, think about the potential of your life and all the good things in it. This power stretch is all about you. Let the demands of everyone and everything else wait.

You may think that such a simple thing won't make a blind bit of difference to how you feel about yourself, but try it once a day for at least three weeks and you'll be surprised. Many sensitive people have fallen into the habit of minimising themselves emotionally, mentally and physically. Your mind is led by your actions just as much as your thoughts, so send it a big message and strike a pose. Notice how liberating and empowering it feels to make yourself bigger than normal and to strike a confident body pose. What you are doing is a physical reminder of your potential strength. The stretch is entirely an act of loving self-care. During the day, notice every time you start to minimise yourself in any way and make a point of correcting your posture and sitting up or standing tall.

Keeping your body constantly hunched and small sends a signal to your brain that you are unimportant and insignificant. Your mind listens to all the messages you send it from your body, so send it a powerful wake-up call every single day. Find the courage to roar!

Sensitivity Code 5: Don't believe it because you think it

You have done the toughest part. You have started to acknowledge and not run away from your inner pain. As you start to better understand who you are and appreciate that your gentleness and sensitivity is not a flaw but a potential gift, you will gradually notice a shift in your thought processes. You will start to see that you have been placing too much store on what others think and not enough on what *you* think. You will stop judging yourself so harshly and feel less of a need to overthink everything in your life.

Thoughts have tremendous power. They can impact our mood, our motivation, our health and well-being. But thoughts only have that power if we allow them to. Just because you think something does not mean it is true. Contrary to what you may have been led to believe, you are *not* what you think. If you think something negative, you don't have to act on that negativity. Thoughts come and go. They emerge from your subconsciousness and can disappear as swiftly as they appeared.

Sensitive people tend to overidentify with their thoughts, assigning them a power over their lives they don't need to have. They can also get into the habit of dwelling on negative things, judgements and anxieties. You need to recast yourself as the witness or observer of your thoughts. They are like a TV signal. You are not that signal. You are the TV that transmits them. Thoughts don't make you feel unhappy. It is only when you start to believe them or identify with them that you suffer.

You are the manager of your thoughts. You choose which thoughts you are going to put the force of your belief behind. You get to decide which thoughts you are going to identify with and act on. Sensitive people tend to get carried away with their thoughts, and they need to remind themselves every single day that their thoughts *do not* define them.

Unlock and take action

This technique should be used every single time your self-talk is harsh, judgemental or negative. Say this in your mind – or even better, out loud: *I am* not *my thoughts. I choose which thoughts to attach to.* Then, as the manager of your thoughts, choose to re-frame negative self-talk in a positive light. Your thoughts impact the way you feel about yourself, so consciously choose empowering self-talk. It will feel odd at first, but keep going.

For example, instead of telling yourself you are too sensitive or emotional, tell yourself that you are inspired by beauty and feelings. Instead of criticising yourself for not being assertive enough, tell yourself it takes courage to be gentle and follow your own path rather than follow ones created and well-trodden down by others. Instead of telling yourself you don't fit in, remember that being true to yourself will attract the right people to you. If you think other people are judging you, tell yourself that you can't control what others think about you. There are always going to be people who don't 'get' you, so let go of the need to impress them. Being authentic and bringing the gentle power and healing of your sensitivity into the world is the purpose of your life. If you think you can't forgive someone, choose to let go of the resentment. If you feel overwhelmed, choose to see this as a sign you need to pay more attention to your own needs. If feel you aren't good enough, choose to see the positive in yourself. You choose!

However, don't think that negative self-talk is ever going to go away completely, because a lot of it is unconscious. You can't stop your thoughts happening any more than you can stop your heart beating, but what you can do is keep your thoughts from taking over. You can learn to identify with your thoughts less, especially when they are negative. One strategy that has proven to be effective is to imagine your negative self-talk coming from a character who instinctively makes you laugh or whom you can't take seriously. The one I always choose is Donald Duck, and every time I think negative thoughts or get overanxious, I hear Donald Duck's voice in my head. If you can laugh at negativity, it often takes away the sting. You may also want to make friends with your negative self-talk and, instead of dreading it, regard it as a sign that you need to be kinder to yourself. See it as a part of you that is hurting, alone and in need of a friend.

Be aware that you are learning a new skill, and like any new skill, this takes practice. You are learning to talk to yourself in a positive and empowering way. Your negative thoughts are not used to being challenged, but if you make a conscious decision to challenge them, it will become second nature in time. You will start to notice when you are losing perspective, seeing only the negative and being unrealistic. You will recognise when you are diminishing your own power. You may also hear a very clear and powerful voice emerge – one that you are familiar with but haven't trusted before – and that is the voice of your inner wisdom, the superpower that is your intuition.

Sensitivity Code 6: Inoculate yourself

Your emotions can be a source of tremendous wisdom and guidance, but just as you are not your thoughts, you are not your emotions either. To lead a successful and fulfilling life, it is important to learn how to manage your emotions, but this can be especially challenging if you are empathetic and prone to taking on or absorbing the feelings of others. Even if you don't score highly on the sensitivity scale, emotions can be contagious, and many of us absorb feelings such as anger, fear and joy from other people without even knowing it. This can explain why sometimes you may feel inexplicably down. You are feeling someone else's pain.

When you feel sad or low, more often than not this is a combination of your own feelings and also what you are absorbing from others around you, so it is important to know how to distinguish between the two. When you feel sad or negative, the first thing you need to do as a sensitive person is ask yourself how much of what you are feeling is yours and how much is coming from an external source. For example, if you always feel low after reading your newsfeed, perhaps you are absorbing negative energies from there. If you always feel drained after spending time in a crowded room or at a certain location, it's likely that you are absorbing negativity there. If you always feel down after interacting with the same person or group of people, they are the likely generator.

One of the reasons many people feel better after interacting with a sensitive person is that a sensitive person can absorb what others are feeling like a sponge. Other people sense your openness to taking on their pain and are more than happy to offload. Keep a record of your moods and see if you can identify a trigger. If what you are feeling isn't yours, use the techniques below to 'inoculate' yourself.

Unlock and take action

This sounds obvious (though all too often most of us miss what is obvious), but if someone makes you feel depressed, avoid spending time with them. If it isn't possible to avoid them because you work with them or they are family members, limit your interactions with them. Seek out people who are supportive and who energise rather than deflate you. This sounds simple, but it isn't easy for sensitive people to detach or let go of toxic relationships or know what is healthy and what is not. Relationships are a key ingredient for happiness and fulfilment in life, but for sensitives they can be a minefield. That's why the next chapter will be devoted to exploring them further and offering more guidance.

For now, this protection-bubble strategy is a fantastic foundation to build on, because protecting your energies from overwhelm or control by others is absolutely crucial for sensitive people to understand themselves, reconnect with their inner power and thrive. When you start to feel sad, negative or vulnerable and you don't think those emotions belong to you but to someone else, take a few deep breaths. Imagine you are breathing out stress and breathing in healing and calm. Then, place one hand gently on your heart and the other on your stomach. These are the two places in your body where negativity can settle, like an unwelcome guest. Send love and healing to your heart and gut by visualising a golden light flooding into them. Then imagine a brilliant white translucent light circling around your body like a protective bubble or an energy catcher that not only allows joy and positivity in but acts like a shield against negativity.

If you find a certain location draining, apply exactly the same strategy. Avoid going there if you can, or physically move to a different location. If you can't do that, limit the amount of time you spend there, and when you do spend time there, put on your protective bubble.

This visualisation technique can be incredibly helpful whenever you encounter anyone or anything that overwhelms you emotionally, but it is so strengthening and empowering that you may also want to consider doing it every single morning when you get up. Spend a few moments after you have got dressed to add an extra layer – your protective bubble or energy catcher.

Sensitivity Code 7: Manage your emotions

Some emotions make you do things or act in a certain way that is damaging to your authentic self. If your feelings are getting in the way of what you want to do with your life or the kind of person you want to be, it is time to take positive action.

Sensitive people often get carried away with emotions in the same way that they can get carried away with their thoughts. Indeed, many feel as if their lives are completely controlled by their emotions. It can be overwhelming at times. If emotions are painful, the temptation to avoid facing them is powerful. The first step is to identify if the emotion is genuinely yours or one you have absorbed from someone else through your empathetic nature. But sometimes the emotions will be your own.

Emotional IQ is important for cracking your sensitivity code. You need to be as in charge of your emotions as you are your thoughts. However, this doesn't mean stifling your emotions; rather it means expressing the full range of your emotions without worrying that they will take you over. If you are emotionally confident you won't say some of the things sensitive people often say. For example: 'I don't know how I feel' or 'I couldn't help or stop myself'. Such statements immediately put you in the role of helpless victim, at the mercy of your emotions.

The very nature of emotions is to be illogical so, unlike your thoughts, instead of questioning or reframing them, you simply need to allow yourself to feel them. This will be painful if the emotions are negative or dark, but every emotion you have is a messenger. The key is to acknowledge your emotions, but not necessarily to act on them. If you don't acknowledge your emotions, this can cause problems, because emotions are messengers from your inner wisdom. If they are not worked through, the biochemical effects of suppressed emotions will lead to physical and emotional poor health. Emotions show what matters to us, and if they are causing us difficulties, this signals the need for some kind of change in our lives. Negative emotions are not bad emotions. They are healthy and necessary for us to grow and develop. Sometimes feeling bad can be good.

Unlock and take action

Whenever you notice that your emotions are taking over or hurting you, remind yourself that they do not define or control you.

Think about what your feelings are trying to tell you. Use the ACM strategy:

Accept: Simply accept what you are feeling. Don't push it away or repress it. Try to understand if the emotion is coming from within you or if it is one that you are absorbing from someone else. If it is coming from within you, try to figure out why, but if there seems to be no reason, simply let the emotion flow through you. If it is an emotion you are absorbing from someone in your life, be aware of that and have the courage to admit the emotion does not belong to you. Set boundaries and apply Sensitivity Code 6 (see earlier in this chapter).

Choose: Decide how you are going to respond to that emotion. Use a tried-and-tested strategy to induce a state of calm. If you feel angry, find a safe way to express it – for example, by punching a cushion. If you feel sad, tears are healing, so find a safe place to cry. If you feel anxious, write down your fears in your journal or a notebook. If you feel lonely, spend time with supportive friends or your pet or in the embrace of nature. If you feel jealous, think about all the things you have to be grateful for in your life. If you feel envy, it's a sign something is missing from your life, so find ways to fill the void. Always try to seek out the positive potential in every emotion. Nothing in life is ever wholly good or bad, including your emotions.

Manage: Remind yourself that *you* are the manager of your feelings. They can't overwhelm you unless you allow them to. Remind yourself, too, that feelings enrich your life. Feelings are messengers of the wisdom of your heart. If you learn to manage your feelings, they can guide and inspire. Feeling something is far more preferable than feeling nothing at all. Being sensitive, you are naturally more in tune with your feelings than other people, which gives you the potential to transform your feelings into a true superpower.

Finally, if you haven't watched the Disney movie *Inside Out*, I urge you to do so, right now. It was nominated for an Oscar and is a masterclass for both adults and children in how to navigate tough emotions successfully. The audience sees that joy can't thrive by itself. Joy needs to understand that sadness, anger and fear should not be repressed and denied. They should be acknowledged and expressed because they play vital parts in growing up, fulfilling relationships, finding inner peace and shaping a resilient person who can cope with whatever life throws at them.

Warning: As with every heartfelt Disney movie, *Inside Out* may make you cry.

Sensitivity Code 8: Master the art of self-love

Despite being some of the most creative, loving, kind and caring people on the planet, the majority of highly sensitive people lack self-worth and struggle to like, let alone love, themselves. There are many reasons for this, and feeling different is one of the major ones, but whatever the reason, if this resonates with you, you will need to tackle this issue head on. To keep on unlocking the sensitivity code, falling in love with yourself is non-negotiable.

Every self-help programme, trend in popular psychology or personal growth movement stresses the vital importance of self-love, but few of them tell us *how* to do actually do that. Many people don't love themselves enough or even know what self-love is. Sensitive people, who care more about the well-being of others than their own, typically haven't got a clue.

Self-love is not consigning yourself to loneliness. Far from it. If you have ever been in an unhappy relationship or felt overwhelmed at a social gathering, you will know that nothing can feel lonelier. Self-love is not feeling lonely regardless of whether you are single or with someone. The actress Emma Watson hit the headlines recently when she was asked about her relationship status. She said she did not consider herself single because she was 'self-partnered', meaning that she was making the choice to love herself.

Self-love is often confused with narcissism, but the two could not be more different. Narcissism is excessive self-centredness, a lack of empathy, an inflated sense of self-importance and entitlement and a need for admiration. A narcissist considers themselves to be of greater value than others. Self-love is taking responsibility for your well-being, realistically accepting your strengths and weaknesses and extending kindness and compassion to yourself. The sensitivity solutions so far have focused on taking responsibility, accepting your strengths and weaknesses, celebrating your uniqueness and challenging negative self-talk. Time now to further complete the puzzle and focus on ways to extend loving kindness and compassion towards yourself.

Warning: Don't be surprised if this solution makes you feel uncomfortable. Sensitive souls have become not only used to placing their own needs last, but also sometimes to not even considering they exist.

Unlock and take action

Learning to love yourself can take time, but you know you are on the right path when you stop comparing yourself negatively to others, worry less about what others think, focus on your strengths rather than your weaknesses, forgive yourself for and learn from any mistakes you make and start saying the word no without feeling guilty.

Many sensitive souls worry about disappointing others or hurting their feelings if they set boundaries and say no. People-pleasing has become a way of life, but this means your kindness is expected and will be exploited. Sooner or later you will feel resentful.

From now on, as you work through the sensitivity codes, try to make a conscious effort to check yourself before you immediately say yes or offer to help someone. If someone asks you to do something you feel you ought to do but don't really want to do, and you can't pluck up the courage yet to say a clear no, tell them you will think about it and get back to them. Let some time go by so they get used to the idea that you aren't immediately available. Then, if they ask again – and they might not, as the chances are they will ask someone else if it is really pressing – tell them gently that you have weighed everything up and right now the answer is no.

You'll be surprised how liberating it is to say the word 'no' if you haven't been saying it for much of your life, and the reason it is empowering is because you are expressing your true feelings or the real you. Loving yourself is expressing your true feelings in a respectful but assertive way. If others can't respect your feelings and are critical of you, then that is their problem and not yours.

Self-love can sometimes feel like a mountain to climb and it will be a work in progress. One way to help you on the journey to knowing your own heart is to keep a journal. Write down any negative feelings and see what you can learn from them. Then, jot down what you have to be grateful for and list your accomplishments. Another way is to wake up every morning and make a self-love promise. The first thought you have in the morning often sets the tone for the entire day ahead, so as soon as you wake up, think of three things about yourself you are grateful for and then make a vow to love yourself. Here's a suggestion for a self-love promise, which you can say today and every morning first thing:

> From now on I pledge to wake up each morning with love for myself. I will ask myself what I need and give myself all that I have. I will take care of myself both when times are good and when times are challenging. I will honour myself and always love and honour the wisdom of my heart. I will be the centre of attention in my own life.

Sensitivity Solution 9: Practise self-care

Self-care plays a crucial part in learning how to love yourself. A lot of sensitive people just do not do self-care, because focusing on their own wants and needs is usually last on their list of priorities, but if you don't practise self-care you are not loving yourself. Self-care is nurturing yourself. It is taking self-loving care of your body, mind, heart and soul every single day, both when you are well and when you are poorly. It is eating healthily, managing stress, exercising regularly and taking the time to recharge when you need it.

Unlock and take action

Everyone practises self-care in their own unique way and you need to find what works best for you. The following self-care tips are not written in stone, but offer you a framework or starting point of self-care essentials to incorporate into your daily life, today and every single day. You will know when your self-care plan is working, as you will feel less stressed, more energised and start to enjoy life more.

- **Eat healthily**. Food is like fuel. If you don't give your car the right fuel it won't run well, and it's the same with your body. Give it what it needs to function at its peak. Research what comprises a healthy diet and which foods are optimum for a healthy brain and body. Nourishing self-care foods include wholegrains, fruit, green leafy vegetables, blueberries, nuts, legumes and fatty fish. Avoid foods and drinks you know aren't healthy for you, though it's okay to enjoy a dessert or glass of wine now and then. As with everything in life, moderation is key.

- **Move it**. Exercise has an impact on your emotional, mental and physical well-being. Commit to at least 30 minutes of movement every day, however busy you are. For example, brisk walking, jogging, cycling, dancing, yoga or swimming. Schedule it into your diary.

- **Sleep on it**. Everything seems better after a good night's sleep. Make sure you get between six and eight hours' sleep a night, and don't burn the candle at both ends. Keep your bedroom free of distractions. If you struggle with sleep, a good bedtime routine can work wonders. This includes no screens an hour or so before bed, drinking herbal tea, reading, a warm bath and other ways to gently unwind. Try to stick to a regular sleeping and waking schedule to regulate your body clock. Bring your bedtime forward 10 to 15 minutes over the week to help you get used to your new bedtime routine.

- **Fresh air**. Make sure you get some fresh air every day, by walking around the block, garden or in your local park, as this will help ease stress and help you sleep better at night.

- **Schedule self-care**. Make sure you plan self-care into your daily routine. This can be as simple as taking some time out to yourself to de-stress by relaxing in a warm bath, to treating yourself to a good book or having a facial. It doesn't matter what it is. The important thing is that it is something that makes you feel good. Keep thinking of ways to balance the needs of your body, mind, heart and spirit, and incorporate more of them into your life.

Sensitivity Code 10: Seek refuge

We all need time out, but when you are sensitive and constantly on high alert, you need far more time out to recover and recharge from the demands of daily life than other people. You also urgently need to spend that downtime alone rather than with other people, because of your tendency to absorb the moods of others and respond to stimuli from the environment you are in.

If you don't get regular alone time to escape from the chaos of life, this will lead to overwhelm. Symptoms of sensory overload include anxiety, lethargy, depression and a loss of concentration, memory and focus, but they can also include physical symptoms, such as sweating, a raised heart rate, an upset stomach, headaches, weight fluctuations, insomnia and fatigue. Seen in this light, seeking refuge on a regular basis is as essential to a sensitive person's health and life as the air they breathe.

Sensitive people are often very busy and productive people, and a part of them may feel guilty taking time out to do nothing in particular. But idle moments help us refresh, step outside ourselves and see the bigger picture. When we return after some time away, we often have a fresh perspective and renewed focus. Busy is not always better. Downtime is essential for your productivity.

If you are a high-energy person, you don't necessarily have to relax during your downtime, you just need to use it to switch off from your thoughts for a while and do something that doesn't involve too much concentration. Downtime is not a waste of time. Indeed, you are more likely to be unproductive if you try to crack on when you feel overwhelmed.

Unlock and take action

Make a conscious decision to spend some downtime alone every day, preferably in the evening. During that time, completely switch off and do nothing in particular. Set aside at least 30 minutes to escape from everyone and everything, especially your mobile phone – switch it to silent and put it away. Use that time to focus on yourself and what you are thinking and feeling. You may turn to music, literature or art during this time, or you may want to spend it in nature or simply meditate or daydream. If you like to keep moving, go for a solitary walk or do some house-work or gardening. It doesn't matter what you choose to do; just find your refuge – a safe place where you can be alone and sim-ply switch off from the demands of others and external stimuli. If you live in a busy household and alone time is not easy to achieve, get up half an hour early, when the house is quiet. To ensure you don't lose out on sleep, be sure to go to bed earlier the night before. Think of that early morning time as your power time, a key ingredient of your happiness and success.

If at any point during your downtime you feel guilty, it might help to think of yourself as a lion lounging in the sun. You are not being lazy, you are simply conserving and recharging your mental and physical energy like a lion, ready to leap back into action when you are refreshed.

Remember, you need to gaze at the trees or the stars to recharge. You need to take long walks, soak for ages in a warm bath or go to bed early to dream or simply lose yourself in a brilliant book. You need regular peace and quiet, just as day needs night. You need your sacred space.

(See Chapter 5 for some essential tips on coping with over-stimulation from your environment.)

Sensitivity Code 11: Find meaning

Over the years I have received hundreds of messages and stories from sensitive souls united by the similarities in their search for higher meaning. I have come to the firm conclusion that the path to fulfilment for gentle folk is through this search for deeper meaning. A sensitive person who defines themselves in terms of their personality, rather than their soul or spirit, is, in my opin-ion, more likely to struggle to find fulfilment in their lives.

Gentle people need to find meaning and purpose in life. This is why they so often struggle with small talk or fail to get excited about material things, such as a new car or a kitchen extension. They need to feel a higher purpose beyond the material or a connection to something greater than themselves. They want their lives to make a difference, and this is the reason you find so many sensitive people doing purposeful work. They are hardwired to see the bigger picture and typically operate in the best interests of the collective, rather than for personal gain. Religion often does not appeal to them because it is too restrictive and they need their freedom of expression, but spirituality or a mystical approach to life can be a path to great fulfilment for sensitive souls.

Unlock and take action

Spirituality is the search for deeper meaning in life. It distracts attention away from the material world to the insights of the wisdom from within. Spiritual practices focus on increasing your feelings of love, compassion, gratitude and forgiveness to discover your meaning and purpose and connect to the highest and wisest part of yourself. This approach to life comes naturally to sensitive souls, but you may have felt ashamed, embarrassed or uncertain about fully embracing your spiritual instincts before, because spirituality is often marginalised in a material world.

Sensitive souls are born with a need to find deeper meaning to their lives (remember, they were the ancient shamans and oracles) and they can never find that meaning in the material. From this day on, make a sacred commitment to your soul to nurture it every single day with spiritual practices that comfort and inspire you. Chapter 7 explores a sensitive person's need to find meaning and how to discover their purpose, but here are a few suggestions to get you started. They are small, daily rituals you can incorporate into your life to help you set positive intentions, bring a sense of inner peace and discover your life's meaning.

- Every day when you get up, say a little prayer. This doesn't need to be a religious prayer, as you don't need to be religious to pray. You don't have to go down on bended knees with folded hands. Simply think of three things that you are grateful for in your life.
- Before each meal or snack, spend a few moments quietly reflecting with gratitude on what you are about to eat.
- Do some cloud-watching or stargazing, or watch the sun rise or set.
- Focus all your attention on the present moment several times a day. If you find your thoughts fast-forwarding to the future or pulling you back to the past, notice them and gently refocus on the present moment and the power of now.
- Go for a mindful walk to clear your head. Or choose an everyday activity, such as brushing your teeth, and do it mindfully, which simply means consciously connecting to what you are doing with all your physical senses.

Sensitivity Solution 12: Simply smile

Saving the best for last, this sensitivity solution is simply going to encourage you to lighten up a little. Sensitive people tend to be a little on the serious side because they are such deep thinkers. From a young age they have often been called old souls or wise beyond their years, and this label has stuck. Their maturity is one of their strengths, but from time to time, it doesn't hurt to take themselves a little less seriously. Laughter truly is the best medicine for sensitive souls carrying the pain of the world on their shoulders.

Life is often no laughing matter. But one of the best ways to empower yourself is to see the lighter side of things. Of course, there are some situations where this isn't appropriate or possible, but in your daily life there are many opportunities to smile more and have fun. This final sensitivity solution encourages you to seek them out.

Unlock and take action

From now on, consciously look for what is positive, hopeful, humorous and inspiring. Seek out things that make you smile on the inside and the outside. Immerse yourself in uplifting music, in the beauty of the natural world or in inspiring art or words as often as you can. Every morning, start your day right with a great big smile and carry that feeling with you during the day. Look at your reflection in a mirror and smile broadly. If you don't feel like smiling, fake your smile. The physical action of smiling actually tricks your brain into thinking you are happier.

Smiling at yourself in the mirror will not only trigger a change in your brain chemistry and mood, but it will remind you that the most important and sacred relationship you will ever have is with *yourself*. You may have got used to looking at yourself over the years in a serious or tense way. So, from now on, whenever you look in a mirror, smile at yourself as if you were meeting someone you love or admire, or someone you want to impress. Light up yourself and your life every single day with your beautiful smile.

Your master PIN

Practised together, these 12 strategies can help you unlock the sensitivity code. They are your master PIN, the secret to a fulfilling and meaningful life. But for them to be effective, you need to incorporate them into every day of your life from now on.

1. **Look within**. Are you seeking validation from others rather than looking internally?
2. **Grow up again**. Are you nurturing your inner child?
3. **Love being different**. Are you celebrating and enjoying who you truly are?
4. **Reach for the stars**. Are you proud of who you are?
5. **Don't believe it because you think it**. Are you observing rather than identifying with your thoughts?
6. **Set boundaries**. Are you prone to taking on or absorbing the feelings of others?
7. **Manage your emotions**. Are you learning from the wisdom of your emotions?
8. **Master the art of self-love**. Are you your own best friend?
9. **Practise self-care**. Are you taking the best care of your physical and emotional health?
10. **Seek refuge**. Have you found your sacred safe place?
11. **Find meaning**. Have you found meaning and purpose in your life?
12. **Simply smile**. Are you seeking what is joyful in your life?

You may want to make a ritual of checking, at the end of each day, how many of these 12 sensitivity solutions you have practised. The ideal is to consistently place a tick beside all 12 of them every single day. They won't make your life perfect, but they will change it for the better and remind you that your gentleness is a strength and not a weakness.

Remember, you need to practise the sensitivity codes for a minimum of three to four weeks before you are likely to experience the benefits and see your life changing for the better. Remember, too, that life is a journey and not a destination. Thinking of your life in terms of a destination means that you are on the wrong track or once again falling into the trap of believing you are somehow different and need to fit in with everyone else who has 'made it'. Whether you are sensitive or not, there are always going to be challenges and setbacks and your life will always be a journey – filled with obstacles, heartaches and hardships, but also joy, surprises and blessings in disguise. Enjoy the ride.

Coming up...

This chapter has focused on the relationship you have with yourself, as this is the most important relationship you will ever have. If your relationship with yourself isn't healthy, nothing in your life will be healthy. But our lives are also defined by our relationships with others, particularly those closest to us, so the subject of Chapter 4 is relationships and sensitive people in love.

CHAPTER 4

Heartfelt

Relationships are a minefield for sensitive souls. As a sensitive, you tend to see the good in other people. You are open-hearted, kind and love to see others thrive. Your generous and kind nature ensures that you are always in demand. So why on earth do you often feel so alone, and even lonelier when surrounded by loved ones, friends and family? Why do sensitive souls, who are hardwired to be loving and giving, often have such complicated relationship histories?

Many of the problems sensitive people have in relationships are caused by their lack of self-awareness and resulting inability to find effective ways to manage their sensitivity. Unlocking and working through the sensitivity code strategies in the previous chapter will help you grow in self-awareness. But there are two people in a relationship. Rather than blaming all problems on yourself, it is important to point out that difficulties can also be triggered by the other person's lack of understanding of your sensitivity, especially your paradoxical need for both closeness and space, sometimes at the same time!

If you don't develop greater self-awareness and your partner doesn't educate themselves about your sensitive nature, over time this will lead to tension. Hopefully, this chapter will help you to resolve such tension and bring healing to all your relationships. And if people who care about you are struggling to understand you, now is the time to encourage them to read this book, starting perhaps with this next section on true love and the things to know if you love a sensitive person.

True love

The right love relationships for sensitives can empower them greatly, but even though it seems all they want is closeness, many also fear true intimacy. They may have been let down so many times in their lives, from childhood onwards, that it feels unsafe to get too close to anyone, even if the other person has their best interests at heart.

Many sensitive souls have learned to wear a mask to hide their sensitivity because they fear being judged or rejected by others. They have learned to shut down their true feelings to the point where pretending becomes second nature. It is hard for others to know exactly what a sensitive person needs or is feeling, and this can create misunderstandings, feelings of isolation within a relationship and lack of authentic connection (also known as attachment trauma) because sensitive people have a habit of letting people get close and then pushing them away.

You may recognise this familiar push and pull. You want, indeed crave, relationships and dream of true love, but then you also want to be alone. It's the same with friendships. You love other people but also crave personal space. You want to be needed but are also resentful if others depend on you too much. You crave closeness but don't want them to get too close.

However much you love or care about a person, spending too much time with them can make you feel anxious. The togetherness overstimulates your empathy. You absorb the emotions of others and this leads to overwhelm, as you are still struggling to deal with your own emotions. The end result is that you have this inexplicable desire to run, even in relationships that are positive for you, like Julia Roberts's character in the movie *Runaway Bride*. She runs away from Richard Gere, who we all know is perfect for her, for goodness' sake!

If you recognise yourself here, I'm willing to bet that you keep on dating or have dated people who are emotionally unavailable. You think there is no one out there for you, but even with someone perfect, chances are you would push them away when the honeymoon phase was over and the time for true intimacy began.

So how can you avoid fear of intimacy in your love relationships?

First of all, you need to seek out people who are available rather than people who have the potential to be available. If someone says they are not ready to commit, believe them. Don't fall in love with what someone could become. Seek out people who are there already. The biggest mistake anyone, sensitive or otherwise, makes in relationships is falling in love with the potential of someone rather than the reality. You have to love people as they are *right now*. If you want connection and intimacy, that's what you need to find in any potential partner from the outset, not in their promises of commitment at some future date. Never put yourself in the position of waiting for someone who is not available to you. You must seek connection, not attachment, to someone.

A sure-fire sign you have found someone who is right for you is that you feel comfortable communicating honestly with them about your needs. You can ask without fearing rejection. If you crave regular periods of solitude or alone time, you need to tell your partner how vital this is to you, so they understand. Decide on how much time together is compatible for you both. If you need physical as well as emotional space, you need to communicate that. Contrary to what you may think, having separate bedrooms is not a sign of a failing relationship. Sometimes it can be the making of it. You also need to talk about how much or how little you enjoy socialising with other people.

If your partner does something that upsets you, tell them in a way that includes positive statements. For example, 'I love you and it would really help me feel less stressed if you remembered to empty the dishwasher.' Above all, don't try to solve your partner's problems or do things for them at the expense of your own needs. Listen to their problems, but respect and empower them by showing that you trust their own ability to solve them.

As far as sex is concerned, sensitive people don't tend to just have sex. They are more likely to make love, and they need to feel the right energy and be in the right mood. If you are having sex with a sensitive person, you will know it is meaningful to them. Casual sex is not typically their modus operandi, although as every sensitive is an individual, it can be for some. They can be deeply sensual, and regular physical intimacy is a big deal to them if they are in love. They are likely to take any kind of physical rejection personally. Their intensity when making love can be intoxicating, but if they are with someone who is less sensual this can cause issues. Again, regular communication with your partner about what you both need to fulfil you sexually is essential.

For a relationship to be fulfilling, it is important that you are as in love with yourself as you are with your partner. That way, if something feels wrong in the relationship, you will assert yourself. Your partner is not telepathic. They need to understand what you need, and the best way for that to happen is for you to *tell them* what you need. If they truly want to be in your life, they will do their best to meet your needs, as you will do your best to meet theirs.

Getting used to the idea that you are worthy of and deserve the love you so readily give others isn't going to happen instantly if you have spent a lifetime feeling the opposite. I truly hope the sensitivity code is already helping you shift your perspective in the right direction.

You may want to starting saying this powerful relationship mantra out loud every morning when you wake up (see Chapter 3 for the reason why this is the optimum time for affirmations): *I deserve to love myself and for others to love me for who I am. I value the power of my gentle heart and I deserve to have people in my life who respect my needs.*

And while you are working on loving yourself so you can love others better, what about the people in your life who love or care for you? You may want to encourage them to review the following suggestions. (Of course, these suggestions also apply to you, as the most important relationship you will ever have in your life is the relationship you have with yourself.)

Things to know about loving or caring for a sensitive person

Falling in love or caring for a sensitive person is an intense and unforgettable experience, and there are important things you need to understand if the relationship is to thrive. Every sensitive soul is unique, but here are some common factors to watch out for.

- As sensitives are so open-hearted and compassionate, people seem to be drawn to them, and you have to get used to sharing them sometimes. Their energy is so welcoming and humble that others want to bask in its warmth as much as you do.
- You need never fear they will betray you, as when they love or care about someone, they are deeply loyal and committed. They put their heart and soul into the relationship and are extremely generous.
- Conflict is something they find distressing and they would rather run away than confront someone.
- Overwhelm is a hazard and they need regular periods of peace and quiet, much preferring an intimate one-on-one than large parties or gatherings. They need lots of

time alone to recalibrate and recharge their emotional resources.

- They are deeply empathetic and often take on your emotions. They can also take on the emotions of other people and will feel inexplicably moody as a result. When they are low, it is not usually you causing the problem but someone or something else.
- They can be passionate to the point of obsession about their ideas or work and manifest great creativity.
- They have a tendency to think in black and white at times, which can be frustrating.
- They need to follow their passions, so don't stop them living their dreams. If they don't feel passionate about what they are doing with their lives, they don't feel alive.
- Decisions are hard for them. They weigh up all the pros and cons and may come across as indecisive, but they fear making the wrong decision and need to think things through.
- They are tough on themselves and extremely self-critical, even though they are very sympathetic towards the mistakes of others.
- They are forgiving but they rarely forget.
- They take any kind of criticism personally. They are so very hard on themselves that if others join in it can really injure them.
- They are terrific listeners and truly interested in what you have to say, often remembering the tiniest detail. Observant, they notice your mood and energy levels instantly, and have an uncanny ability to see what is really going on.
- They need honesty and openness in their relationships.
- Insomnia is common because their minds are very active, so helping them to find peace and calm, and a good night's sleep, is important.

- Because they love so deeply, they find it hard to let go and process their emotions when a relationship has run its course. Heartbreak hits them harder than others. Be careful. Be gentle with their hearts.

Name your five

It has often been said that the five people you spend the most of your time with shape your life and say a great deal about you – far more than you realise. Many sensitives don't have a relationship filter. They welcome everyone with open arms and hearts. While their openness, trust and generosity are endearing qualities, these can also be a source of great internal and external conflict. Their reluctance to say no, or express what they really feel for fear of upsetting anyone, means many of their relationships are one-sided, with them doing all the giving.

Being selective with relationships and friendships is important for everyone, but it is crucial for sensitives, given their openness and tendency to absorb the emotions of others. If you have a history of complicated and painful relationships, learning how to attract people you admire (and who admire you in return) and avoid people who are going to drain you is necessary for your success and happiness.

Try this exercise: Write down the names of the five people you spend most of your time with. It's best to focus only on adults here, rather than children. If you spend most of your time with your children, think about the adults you interact with the most. If you struggle to think of five people, list who you can, even if it's only two or three people. Don't be tempted to simply list the names of the people you feel closest to or care about the most. Write down who gets most of your time and attention. Ask yourself if these people represent things that you truly admire and love. Ask yourself, too, if these relationships are one-sided or reciprocal. In other words, is there a balance between giving and taking?

Be honest with yourself here. If you don't feel that these people raise you up or return your devotion in equal measure, it is time to get strategic with your relationships. As you continue to work through this chapter and learn more about sensitive love – what works and what doesn't – you may want to re-evaluate the people who take up the majority of your time or find ways to bring greater balance into your relationships with them.

Co-dependence, people-pleasing and an addiction to helping others at the expense of your own well-being often have their origins in childhood. Somewhere along the way you may have learned from your parents or carers that love was conditional rather than unconditional. You only felt loved when you behaved in a certain way or did something your parent or carer wanted, and if you deviated from what they required or wanted, you were rejected. Most parents and carers discipline their children, but not in such a way that they don't feel loved if they don't do what is expected.

If there was an absence of unconditional love in your early life and you are a sensitive person, the chances are that you will be drawn into co-dependent and people-pleasing relationships like a moth to a flame.

Do unto others?

Sensitivity Code 8 (see Chapter 3) stressed the vital importance of self-love in order for a sensitive person to discover their true power. Self-love is also vital for fulfilling relationships. If you are a sensitive person, the concept of self-love is a challenge, and even if you understand why it is essential, you will likely always need to make a conscious effort to observe it, because your default position is to give. You have probably always placed a higher value on the love you can give to others. This is especially the case if you were brought up in a religious or spiritual household that stressed the importance of compassion.

This was certainly my experience. In my late teens I fell in love with Christianity. I seriously considered becoming one of the first female priests or even joining a holy order. My mother was a nun for five years in the Order of St Francis, before she left that life. The Christian message of doing unto others as you would be done unto, turning the other cheek and giving unconditional love for others spoke directly to me. I still identify with that beautiful ideal to this day, but while at university, I was introduced to teachings from other religions and I recognised the beauty in them all. They all resonated with me. It was a major shift and the beginning of my journey towards understanding that there is a difference between religion and spirituality.

Today, I think of myself as a spiritual person attached to no particular religion, but even though I have left my Christian upbringing behind, the message to treat others as I would like to be treated myself and to always put others first is ingrained. I truly did try to live by those ideals. It took me decades to learn that, in the majority of cases, people don't treat you as you treat them. Just because you approach a relationship with love, trust and a willingness to give and share selflessly does not mean the other person is going to return or match your commitment.

What I learned through bitter experience was that people treat you as you treat yourself. If you don't value, respect or love yourself, the people you attract into your life will mirror your lack of self-love back to you.

Like seeks like

In the last few decades, even though there is plenty of anecdotal but no scientific evidence to validate it, the power-of-positive-thinking movement has thrust into the spotlight the so-called Law of Attraction, which draws its inspiration from quantum theory and the suggestion that we are all made up of vibrational energy waves. According to Law of Attraction theory our thoughts are also vibrational energy waves that impact the energy fields around us. Like magnets, we attract into our lives whoever or whatever is on a similar vibrational energy frequency to us – in other words 'like seeks like'. So, if your thoughts are negative or you dwell on what you *don't* want, that's exactly what will manifest in your life. Your consciousness creates your world. However, if you reframe your thoughts and focus on what you *do* want, the universe will attract the right people and the success you dream of to you. It all sounds so easy, doesn't it! Dream and it will manifest. But as you have probably found, if you've tried this approach, it isn't quite that simple.

Perhaps, along with millions of others, you have tried to utilise the power of positive thinking. You have read books like the million-selling positive-thinking bible *The Secret* by Rhonda Byrne and have tried to work with the Law of Attraction, but have given up because it didn't change your life or your relationships for the better. In fact, it just made you think that you had failed again or you must have got your thinking all wrong!

If the theory that you can think your way to a better life and more fulfilling relationships sounds too good to be true, that's because it is. You can't simply *think* your way to a better life. The Law of Attraction doesn't respond to your thoughts so much as to what you *feel* passionately about, and then what you choose to actually *do* in response to your feelings. And your feelings have their roots in what you believe to be true about yourself. So if you believe yourself to be flawed or that you don't deserve to be loved for who you are, your relationships and your life in general will reflect that sense of disappointment back to you.

That sense of worthlessness will be reflected back to you in your career or what you do with your life. I'm a case in point myself. When I left King's College, Cambridge, instead of using the wonderful opportunity my degree gave me to apply for internships or graduate positions, I devoted my post-university years to teaching keep-fit classes full-time. My classes were popular in London and it was wonderful to help people feel better about themselves, but it took one of my clients to point out to me that I didn't really need a Cambridge degree to be a fitness instructor for me to actually do something about it.

Your own feelings of inadequacy will be reflected back to you in your health and well-being. If you love yourself, you are going to take good care of yourself and make self-care a priority. You may know this to be true already in that when you feel happy, you don't usually get sick. Illness tends to strike when you feel stressed and aren't looking after yourself.

Your feelings of self-worth will be reflected in the friendships you have. You will find yourself surrounded by friends who don't reciprocate your depth of friendship, and you will see this reflected most acutely in your close relationships. This rule doesn't apply in cases where love is unconditional, such as the love young children have for their parents, and the unconditional love parents often have for their children, whatever age they are, but if you don't love yourself, the people you choose to love or associate with won't value you.

To change your life for the better, you have to change the way you feel about yourself *first* and then take action to prove that what you feel about yourself is genuine. If you want to get a sense of just how much you love yourself, the place to find the answer is in your close relationships. The quality of those relationships will mirror the value you place upon yourself.

However positively you think about or visualise having supportive and loving relationships, if you don't value, love and honour yourself you won't attract positive relationships into your life. If people consistently treat you with love and respect, chances are you are treating yourself with love and respect. No relationship is ever perfect, and there will always be some kind of tension and conflict, but if, on balance, you feel valued and respected by other people, you are on the right track. However, if you constantly feel let down, disappointed or drained after your interactions with others, this is a big red flag. Your self-love tank is running on empty.

People who love themselves are cautiously optimistic about who they allow into their life. They take their time to trust people and don't become intimate with them too soon. If someone repeatedly lets them down and belittles them, and the relationship is not reciprocal, they will not continue the relationship. If they can't avoid seeing that person again because they are dealing with a close family member, then they will find ways to manage that relationship so that it does the minimum of damage to their self-esteem. The love they have for themselves dictates the quality of their relationships.

If you think you want supportive and loving people in your life but always seem to attract the opposite, the way to create change is not to seek out new relationships. The place to begin is within your heart. You need to fall in love with yourself first, because once you do that you simply won't allow negative people to take advantage of your good nature. You won't allow people who take but rarely, if ever, give into your life any more.

Give and you shall not receive

The principle of 'like seeks like' responds to your level of self-worth. Sensitive souls who place a low value on themselves often don't attract other selfless people who validate them into their lives. They may instead attract self-centred or narcissistic people who mirror the way they feel about themselves and devalue them.

Just as your default position is to fall into the role of giver, listener and helper, there are also people whose default position is to fall into the role of taker. It's not always easy to spot these people, because on first meeting they can appear so charming or vulnerable. They seem to understand you completely and think the entire world of you. Intimacy develops very quickly – in a matter of hours sometimes. The flattery is delightful and if the relationship is potentially a romantic one, there is talk of being soulmates.

Trusting and open-hearted as you are, what you may not realise is that while the budding friendship or relationship may feel real to you, what is really happening is that you are being love-bombed by a narcissist or, as a I prefer to call them, an energy vampire. Once the love-bomb stage is over and the sensitive soul has emotionally bonded, the energy vampire will then suddenly withdraw their interest and affection without explanation. This is painfully confusing to the sensitive. They find themselves bending over backwards to try to recapture the golden phase of their relationship, thinking they must have done something wrong. Traumatised and searching for answers, they will never believe they are now helpless and caught in the energy vampire's toxic web. The relationship, if you can call it that, is totally one-sided, with the sensitive doing all the giving and the vampire drinking everything in.

Sensitive souls are the fuel of choice for energy vampires. If they aren't educated about the existence of such unempathetic people and don't realise that nothing they do or say will change the relationship dynamic, they can be trapped for years, even decades, in co-dependent relationships, hoping the other person will one day see their worth. The abuse is typically emotional, but it can also be physical.

If you aren't aware of the phenomenon of narcissistic abuse, which is now more openly discussed and highly visible on social media, I truly hope this book opens your eyes to this modern curse, so that you never have your beautiful energy and goodwill drained by a narcissist again.

A few years ago, I received a crash course in narcissism, and I will share my personal story in the hope it will enlighten other unsuspecting sensitive souls. After that I will offer advice on how to spot the red flags of an energy vampire, what to do if you suspect you are in a relationship with one and how to heal the deep pain it can cause your sensitive heart.

Sweet-talking

As a sensitive person, my life has always been guided and inspired by love, kindness, compassion and empathy. Seeing the light in everyone and everything and being sensitive to the needs of others is the spiritual path I urge my readers to walk. I simply could not have written all the books I have about spirituality without believing that spiritual approach to be true. But the sad truth is that six years ago my belief that the power of love could explain and conquer all was shaken to its core.

Six years ago, someone jumped into my professional life with a powerful endorsement from a trusted source. I had no reason to doubt them, but over the next two years I glimpsed hell on earth. The story is a long one – a book in itself – so I won't share it here. Suffice to say I experienced the pain, confusion, emptiness and heartbreak that people involved with narcissists endure. I'd never encountered someone before who flattered with such intensity, who believed in their own magnificence so completely and who had such incredible ideas and vision... but who also deceived with such relish, played with the truth so nobody knew what was real any more, took greedily without any thought of giving back and whose promises meant absolutely nothing.

Despite the harrowing intensity of the confusion and pain, and the obvious red flags, instead of valuing myself enough to walk away, I went into denial. I found myself inexplicably trying to do all I could to help, support or impress them, so the person I thought they were could return. The initial golden period of adoration had been harshly replaced with silent treatments and gaslighting (which is making someone doubt their own experiences and sanity so you don't know what is true any more). I believed that by showering them with understanding and kindness, they would change or see my worth again, but the more I gave of myself, the worse things got. It was pitiful. I was lost.

Being a spiritual author, people often write to me asking for advice about why bad things happen, or for my spiritual guidance on dealing with the loss of a loved one or a crisis of belief in themselves. I care deeply about my readers and love nothing more than to teach, share my knowledge and see others grow, but during that dark period in my professional life, I found myself, for the first time, simply unable to offer that guidance with any conviction. I could not understand how someone who appeared to be so perfect and so supportive of me, and in whom I had believed so completely, could be so deceptive.

The reason I couldn't respond with conviction to my readers at that time was because I needed help and understanding myself, having encountered a narcissist so up close and personal. Like most sensitives, asking anyone – even family and friends – for help doesn't come naturally to me. On this occasion I needed help urgently, so I did what I always do – I prayed. And in time, courtesy of Google, I found the help I needed. In my desperate search for answers I stumbled across the term 'narcissistic abuse' for the first time. What I found out was a revelation. I was so grateful for the expert advice I found that I reached out to one of the leading online experts in narcissistic abuse, Melanie Tonia Evans. It was an absolute joy when that connection eventually led to Melanie publishing her first book. I had the honour of writing a preface[24] for that book and recording a YouTube video with her[25].

---

24 Evans, M.T. (2018) *You Can Thrive After Narcissistic Abuse*. Watkins.

25 https://www.youtube.com/watch?v=-LtnEfrFHTs

Five years on, I'm at the end of the narcissistic tunnel and have reached the point where I'm actually grateful for the experience, because it showed me that even though I thought I was making progress and setting clear boundaries with others in my life, there was still a way to go in the self-love department. The experience taught me something I instinctively knew but clearly needed to be reminded of, and that was that the validation, adoration and vision I was seeking outside myself were all things I needed to discover from the inside out. I have also reached a point of truly not wanting to seek understanding or revenge, because I know the law of karma will deal with them. I can let go and simply send them love and hope they find their peace.

Of course, I'm saying all this with the benefit of hindsight, because at the time, understanding seemed impossible. That's why this book feels like such an important one for me to write; I hope it will be a wake-up call for every sensitive person who reads it. Even if you are growing in self-awareness, your trusting and gentle nature is one that will attract toxic people who want to take advantage or feed on the attention they extract from you.

Whether or not you have suffered from narcissistic abuse, narcissistic personality disorder is out there and sensitive, empathetic people are the narcissist's drug of choice. If you haven't encountered a narcissist yet, chances are you will, if you are a sensitive person.

Encountering narcissists

They are charming, but you notice they expect special treatment and are hypersensitive to criticism. They reel you into a relationship by making you think you are the perfect match for them or they have the answers to all your questions or needs. Then they use subtly destructive methods of emotional control, like gaslighting, to shred your self-confidence. The most dangerous narcissists will go to any lengths to manipulate, abuse and ultimately discard unsuspecting victims, feeling no remorse.

Sensitive people who aren't aware of the warning signs are totally unprepared to deal with them. In the last ten years, clinical diagnosis of narcissistic personality disorder has risen as quickly as rates of obesity, and people with NPD are estimated to comprise up to one percent of the population (although as they are unlikely given their personality traits to present for diagnosis, the true figure is likely to be way higher). These undiagnosed people are at large in society, leaving trails of misery in their wakes.

Narcissists portray an image of overconfidence to the world to cover up feelings of deep insecurity and fragile self-esteem inside. And even though they appear to be polar opposites, in this respect they are similar to sensitive souls who also often lack self-esteem. Whereas the sensitive tries to find wholeness through people-pleasing, the narcissist seeks it through a constant need for attention. That is why people are disposable for them. They go wherever there is attention. Even if the attention is negative, they still feed on it. Being the centre of attention is everything.

Some experts believe that narcissists are actually sensitive people who have experienced such emotional abuse or trauma in their childhood that they made a dark choice to kill off their sensitivity and empathy. But whatever the reason narcissists exist, it is likely you will encounter these cunning manipulators every day. In broader culture, with the blatant, aggressive self-centredness and lying of politicians, 'selfie' culture and social media self-promotion, which, in my opinion, all appears to suggest that fame, material wealth and celebrity should be prized above all else, we are seeing a perfect storm of narcissism and risk this personality trait being normalised, even celebrated, while gentleness and kindness are marginalised.

Fortunately, sensitive people are becoming educated about the dangers of encountering narcissists, and this welcome development is largely thanks to an incredible online community of survivors sharing their knowledge. Do check out the resources for some recommendations. I hope this book will play a part in raising awareness so that you can spot a narcissist early on and either avoid them or keep contact to a minimum.

Red flags

The early stages of a relationship or friendship with a narcissist feel like nothing you have encountered before. It is only with hindsight that you can recognise the red flags you didn't spot at the time. My experience with the narcissist who traumatised my life ticked all the red flag boxes below.

- **Intense flattery**. This person absolutely adores you or your work, or something you do or have, and very soon you find yourself responding to that flattery by sharing intimate details you normally wouldn't share with anyone but close family and friends. Later you discover that they had an agenda because they wanted something from you, be that contacts, endorsement, sex, money or similar. Once they get what they want, the flattery stops.
- **Their actions don't match their words**. This person promises you everything but there always seem to be a convincing reason why they don't deliver. They are also prone to wild exaggeration. Despite all evidence to the contrary, you believe them, because that is what sensitive people do – they are trusting souls and think others are, too.
- **Zero empathy**. A lack of care and consideration that doesn't match their intense flattery, such as taking calls from other people while leaving you on hold. Once they sense that you are 'caught', their lack of empathy be-

comes more apparent and transforms into manipulation and belittling, as they move on to their next conquest.

- **Focus on status**. This person thinks they should only be surrounded by high-status people and by the very best. Everything about them is 'the best'. For a sensitive person with low self-esteem, the fact this 'accomplished' person has chosen you is very seductive – until they discard you and make you feel like dirt.
- **Entitlement**. This person thinks they are special and should be the centre of your world, despite declaring at the beginning that you are the centre of theirs.

Reading that list, you may wonder how on earth someone can be so gullible as to not recognise the obvious red flags of narcissism sooner, but people who are sensitive, trusting and not fully self-aware are easy prey for such skilled manipulators. This is especially the case if the relationship is sexual, because sexual energy can cloud judgement. Narcissists are often extremely charismatic and expert flatterers, and in the early stages are like wolves in sheep's clothing. They appear as anything but a narcissist to draw you in.

If you have low self-esteem and encounter someone who embodies the assurance and accomplishment you feel you lack, and that perfect person shows interest in you, it is an intoxicating brew. You may also feel that you don't deserve to be treated with respect, and if anything does cause you anxiety, you may not have the confidence to raise it for fear of alienating them. Last but by no means least, if you were born into a family where your needs were not met or you were not loved unconditionally, the narcissist may feel somehow 'familiar' and you might find yourself drawn to that familiarity.

The attraction between sensitive, empathetic souls and narcissists is strong. But unlocking the sensitivity code will help you to instantly spot and avoid someone who is self-serving and does not have your best interests at heart.

What to do if you are in a relationship with a narcissist

I don't believe in hell, but being in a relationship with or getting tangled up with a narcissistic person feels very close to it, and it is particularly harrowing for sensitive souls because they feel things so intensely. Fortunately, there can be life after narcissistic abuse and the first place to look for this understanding and healing is within.

If you are in a relationship with a narcissist or an energy vampire and unable or unwilling to leave even though it makes you unhappy, this is a clear sign that your self-love tank is running on empty and you have trauma-bonded with the narcissist. You still believe that your happiness lies in relationships or external forces and you are looking for the narcissist to 'complete' you.

Unlocking the sensitivity code and applying those strategies to your life every single day will help you find the courage and self-love you need to cease contact with a narcissist. In time, you may even find, as I do now, that the moment someone crosses your boundaries or does not treat you with consideration, you take immediate steps to eliminate them from your life, or to protect yourself if contact is unavoidable. Going no contact can be especially hard if you are a co-dependent and think your love and care can somehow transform the narcissist. What you need to realise is that sadly there is no cure for narcissism. Nothing you say or do will ever make them have empathy for you, because they have no empathy and do not know how to love. Sadly, in their case, the only way love can conquer all is for you to give the love you are wasting on them to yourself.

Armed with self-love, you will no longer tolerate lack of care and consideration from anyone. If it is a family member or a colleague or a boss who behaves narcissistically and you can't cease contact with them, you will find ways to release your emotional attachment to them and keep contact to a minimum. You will find a way to protect yourself and to put your needs centre stage. If you can't imagine yourself finding that kind of courage, just keep unlocking the sensitivity code for at least three weeks. See if you feel the same way after that.

The more I grow in self-awareness and self-love, the more I am repelled by rather than attracted to narcissists. If I do have to interact with a narcissist or energy vampire, they also sense that I am no longer susceptible to their manipulation and flattery. For me, that is one of the most powerful things about unlocking the sensitivity code. My default position is still to trust other people and see the good in them until proven otherwise, but the moment I spot a red flag, I pay attention. I have also learned not to believe what someone says but what someone does. When people show me who they are, I believe them. And when someone reveals who they are through lack of consideration, I no longer make excuses for them or blame myself but accept how they are. I would rather be alone than in the company of energy vampires. This doesn't mean I have become selfish and no longer give or help others; it means I insist on there being a healthy balance in every one of my relationships.

Essential balance

A certain amount of selfishness is not evil or bad and that is the lesson narcissistic people, as draining as they are, can teach us. Indeed, it is healthy to be a little selfish from time to time. Narcissists simply carry their selfishness to extremes, just as sensitives carry their selflessness to extremes. The key to relationship happiness is to find that essential balance.

Self-love is not something that can be achieved overnight – indeed, for many of us it is a lifetime's journey. So, if you are just beginning your journey, what can you do immediately to repel energy vampires and start attracting more positive people into your life?

To risk repeating myself, you need to focus with passion every day on unlocking the sensitivity code. All 12 strategies in the previous chapter will help you become as compassionate to yourself as you already are to others and find that essential balance between giving and receiving.

Sensitive people are highly developed givers, but more often than not, they have no idea how to receive with grace. Simon, who is one of my readers, wrote the following to me and it is something I have often heard sensitive people say.

> If I am given a gift I actually feel uncomfortable. It is such a strange sensation, and my usual response is to either hand the gift back or insist on paying, or I will go out of my way to repay them in some other way. Why do I find it so easy to give and so very hard to receive? I'm the same with compliments – I can't accept them either.
>
> Simon, 17

The reasons for feeling uncomfortable with receiving may date back to childhood, when the sensitive person fell very quickly into the role of family caregiver or helper, but whatever the reason, learning how to receive with grace is important if you wish to restore balance in a relationship. Allowing others to give to you and simply saying 'thank you' if someone pays you a compliment, instead of brushing it aside, is an indication that you believe you are worth giving to and complimenting.

Unlocking the sensitivity code will also help you learn to assert yourself in your relationships, create healthy boundaries and receive with grace. If you aren't sure where to begin, start small. For example, if you have a friend who keeps calling you late in the evening and you really value peace and quiet in your evenings, tell them that you won't be taking calls after seven p.m., or any time that feels right for you. If they ignore that request and still contact you late at night, this is a red flag. This person has not respected your boundaries. People who don't respect your boundaries don't respect you. However, if you haven't told them you don't want to be called late, and still answer their call, you can't expect them to change. You need to tell your friend what you do and do not feel comfortable with.

When you start to say what you mean rather than what is expected of you and let others prove they are worth your time and attention, you will know that you are finding that essential balance for fulfilling relationships. Kindness is your strength and you will always be one of life's givers, but moving forward, if you know that helping will make you feel resentful or depleted, tone down the helping.

Indeed, sometimes not helping is actually helping. The problem with always helping people is that it can make others dependent on you. With you always there to aid them, they never learn to function independently. Remember, the greatest gift you can give yourself and others is self-belief. Sometimes the best gift you can give someone is not jumping in to help but stepping back and letting them find their own solutions.

You can't force other people to love or like you by always being there for them. If you fear that not helping means you will lose them, think about it this way: if someone only wants you around because you make their life easier, is that really a relationship? Fulfilling relationships are not about two people needing each other but about two people choosing to spend time together because it is empowering for both of them.

It's really not always about you

Blessed with a sixth sense about what people are really thinking and feeling, sensitive souls are remarkably good at reading people. But just because you are intuitive about other people's motivations does not mean you are always right. Your tendency to overanalyse and personalise even the most casual of interactions means you can also get things very wrong. This story sent to me by Charlie about a 'disagreement' she had with a close friend demonstrates this perfectly.

Theresa, I like to think I can sense the motivations of others. I'm really attuned to changes in mood and atmosphere and I pride myself on reading my friends like a book. I can tell when they are happy or sad by their body language and tone of voice. I'm often spot on and my family called me 'psychic' because I seem to read their thoughts. However, a recent experience taught me that I can sometimes assign far too much significance to what I believe I'm sensing about someone and not enough to common sense. Here is what happened. I was walking down the street and I saw a good friend of mine on the other side of the road. I waved to her and called out her name. She looked in my direction but did not return the wave and walked on. It really shook me. For days afterwards, I worried if I had somehow offended her. I played our last phone call over and over in my mind to see if there was anything I had said or done to upset her and I couldn't think of anything. I thought about giving her a call or sending her a text but worried that this would make things worse. She had ignored me for a reason. It was so unlike her.

A week later we both went to a party thrown by mutual friends. When I got there, I saw my friend and waved – and once again got the cold shoulder. The party was ruined from that moment on. I made my excuses and left early. Later that evening I got a text from my friend asking if I was okay. I didn't reply because I didn't know what to say. There was nothing wrong with me. She was the one who had been ignoring me!

The following week my friend called me up and asked me what was going on. I blurted out how rejected I had felt ever since she ignored me when I was out shopping. She laughed and said she was ignoring everyone at the moment because she'd had an eye infection and couldn't wear her contact lenses. She said she hated wearing spectacles. She had heard her name called that day and had looked around, but dismissed it as coincidence because she couldn't see the faces of people clearly from across the street. At the party she had still been suffering from her eye infection but had been looking forward to seeing me. She had texted me to ask if I was okay because it was so unlike me to leave before saying hello to her.

If I had simply picked up the phone or sent a text and asked my friend why she hadn't waved back when I had waved to her, I could have saved myself a heap of heartache. I had let my anxiety and willingness to believe the worst-case scenario override my common sense. She hadn't ignored me by choice. She simply hadn't been able to see me.

Charlie, 52

I also feel this story sent to me by Daniel makes a valid point.

My girlfriend became very distant and I couldn't understand why. I was convinced I had done something to offend her or that she was falling out of love with me. I'm ashamed to admit it but I even tried to unlock her phone to see if she was having an affair. Every time I asked her, she said she was fine and was simply feeling pressured by work, but it was clear to me that she was not fine. It made me feel very anxious as I loved her very much and, although we had only been together for a few months, I was thinking of proposing. She was the one!

Then one day she sat me down and told me she was pregnant. She had been thinking about whether to have an abortion for the last few weeks and not tell me anything, because she didn't want to lose me. You see, when we first met we had spoken about kids and I had said I hated them. I was actually joking. I don't hate kids, I just find them very noisy and chaotic and I love my peace and quiet. But this didn't mean I didn't want to consider having any of my own. She had taken what I was saying to heart and had been rigorous with her birth control as a result. She was terrified I might think she was trying to trap me into marriage.

I nearly cried with relief when she told me, and then she started crying herself because, of course, I proposed.

Daniel, 36

The next time you find yourself fretting and overanalysing people or events, remind yourself it is entirely possible that the reason someone said or did something has nothing to do with you and everything to do with what is going on in their own lives. Remember, the sensitivity code stresses the importance of not believing everything you think and feel. This is especially the case for sensitive people and their relationships. You think or feel something and immediately assume you must have done something wrong. What you need to understand is that often it is not about you at all. The focus of most people's lives is what is going on for them. Remember this, moving forward in all your interactions. What people say and do isn't all about you! It's all about them. In the next chapter, we'll further explore the transformative power of taking what other people say and do less personally, using the art of detachment.

The joys of solitude

You may well find, as you start to reflect on the quality of your relationships and work through and implement the self-love suggestions offered in this chapter, that your phone rings and beeps less or that your social calendar isn't as crowded as before. Treat this as a positive sign, as it shows that you are growing personally and may in the process be outgrowing certain people in your life, becoming more selective in your relationships.

> Ever since I started to work on self-care and asserting myself, I have encountered nothing but resistance from people I thought were my friends. A case in point is one of my oldest friends. We were inseparable at school and have kept in touch ever since. Now we are in our twenties with jobs and families. We had got into a pattern of phoning each other every few days and meeting at least once a month, but in recent years I have increasingly had to travel to my friend to meet her, rather than the other way around. She said she couldn't come to me due to work and family commitments. I have a busy life too, but I went along with this for a year or so, and then last month I had a bout of flu, which upset my schedule. So I asked my friend if she could make the effort to come to me this time. She said she couldn't and didn't even suggest ever travelling to me. I then realised that our friendship was based on me making all the effort, so gradually I contacted her less. She noticed this and got in touch, saying that she didn't understand why I was angry with her. I explained that I wasn't angry, I just needed there to be more give and take. She told me I was crazy and hung up. This was my best friend of 20 years! Theresa, it hurt me so much and makes me wonder if the friendship was ever real in the first place.

This isn't an isolated incident. I have noticed the same pushback from other friends, colleagues and even family members. It is tough, and at times I feel I should revert back to my people-pleasing ways to make them happy, but it's simply impossible for me to do that now. I have learned too much. I feel like I am not respecting myself if I do that. I have far fewer friends now, but the people who are in my life are ones who don't take more than they give. I've never felt happier with less.

Lisa, 27

Although sensitive people are blessed with a rich inner life and cope with solitude far better than others, it can feel alarming at first to spend more time alone than before. If increased time on your own makes you feel anxious, remind yourself that this is a sign you need to do more work on the inner you and you are still looking outside yourself to others for validation. Of course, relationships are a source of tremendous fulfilment, but it truly is better to be alone than with people who don't value you. Use your increased time alone to practise self-care and nurture inner growth.

Parties, social events and gatherings have their place, yet a great deal of what goes on is superficial. Once you understand that being 'seen' or admired or noticed is not a path to true fulfilment or friendship, you'll realise that you don't have to accept every invitation. Go if you genuinely enjoy it, but if you hate small talk and superficial chat, as most sensitive souls do, politely decline. You don't need to be there!

Want but don't need

Whenever you operate from a position of need there is always dissonance. Here's an example from my own life.

In 2019 I took a leap of faith and launched my own podcast, *White Shores*. The idea was to invite scientists and leaders in spiritual thought to talk about the science of consciousness and personal growth. I invited the scientists I admire, and to my delight they agreed. I also invited bestselling authors and experts. I recorded all the interviews and loved every minute. One of the interviews was with none other than Pixar co-founder Loren Carpenter, who is also an extraordinary scientist working in the field of consciousness research. I was nervous in that interview, as this incredible man – an Oscar winner – was behind some of the films that had defined my life. Listening back afterwards, I cringed a little inside, as I was gushing and saying 'wow' a lot. Loren was remarkably gracious though.

Emboldened by the success of the interviews I had done – remember, I'm an author, not a podcaster or an interviewer – I decided to reach out to a person who had recently endorsed one of my books, Deepak Chopra. I don't agree with everything Chopra writes or states, but some of his books are iconic and he is one of the world's most famous figures in the field of spirituality. I could not believe my good fortune when he agreed. Having Chopra's name attached to the podcast would be incredible PR for the scientists and their consciousness research, which the podcast was designed to promote.

Nerves kicked in as the interview date crept closer, compounded by the fact that Chopra's team assigned me only 20 minutes and wanted me to record a phone call with him rather than utilise the podcasting recording app I had been using. I have never taped a phone call before and struggle with technology at the best of times, but eventually I was good to go and the interview happened.

During the interview I was once again very nervous, but we did manage to have a fairly decent conversation. When the 20 minutes was over, I was eager to relive the moment and share it with my readers via my podcast, but when I hit play I got 20 minutes of silence. In my nervous state, I had not thought to change the settings from the UK to the US, where Chopra is based. I immediately got in touch with them to ask if we could do the interview again, but they politely declined, saying his schedule was too busy.

The disappointment hit me hard, and even though I had recorded some fascinating interviews, for a brief time I lost my enthusiasm for the podcast. But then I had an aha moment. There was a life lesson in all this. I had approached my interview with Chopra from a state of need and feeling 'less than' or inferior, and whenever you do that there is going to be dissonance. (Not that this applies to sensitives, but do be aware that there will also be dissonance if a situation is approached feeling 'more than' or superior, as we are all equal.) So, I decided to turn a negative into a positive and included the story of my Deepak interview disaster in the episode with Loren Carpenter. Indeed, that episode has become one of the most popular, because pre and post interview I reflect on my interview mistakes both with Loren, and the insecure nerves I felt with Chopra, to highlight the dangers of feeling 'less than'. And I need not have worried about the podcast tanking without Deepak's star turn. To date, my podcast has had several thousand downloads, and the amazing scientists and sensitive souls I interviewed have been warmly received. My readers didn't need the lure of a celebrity to entice them to listen.

Every time I think I have learned an important lesson, life throws another one at me, so I can learn more and grow again. I know it will be the same for you. Look at all the mistakes and disappointments in your own life not as failures but as *lessons* – there to teach you something valuable about yourself and to remind you that you don't need other people to validate you. You are not less than or more than anyone else. We are all equal.

It is so sad when you look at social media these days. It seems everyone is crying out for other people to validate them. The next time you see people posting, don't think they have it all or are better than you. Think about why they need to be doing this. The only validation you need is that which comes from the inside out. People who feel good about themselves don't need to convince others that they are feeling good about themselves. If you are on social media and feel compelled to post endless updates to impress or keep up with others, try posting a little less and believing in yourself a little more.

Self-belief is the hardest journey, and sensitive people seem to take longer than others to believe in themselves. But the only person you need to impress is yourself and the only person you need to compare yourself with is the person you were yesterday.

Relationships are mirrors and teachers

As you work though the sensitivity code and start believing in your own power more, keep a close eye on what happens with all your friendships and relationships. When they start to improve, you know you are making progress. You may even find that the list of five people I urged you to create at the start of this chapter changes. Remember, don't beat yourself up if you make mistakes and people turn out not to be what they seemed. Relationship disappointments happen to everyone, whether they are sensitive or not, and there is no such thing as a perfect relationship. However, if you are learning to harness the power of your gentleness, you will have the resources to forgive yourself, learn from any mistakes you make and let go with love and gratitude for the lessons it has taught you of any relationship that is no longer empowering you. People come into your life for a season, meaning they are passing through and the bond is sharing similar experiences to you – or for a reason, meaning you work together or have something to teach each other – or for life. The people who care about you for life are extremely rare; most relationships are for a season or a reason and you need to get used to enjoying them while they last.

The sensitivity code teaches you that every person who comes into your life is both a mirror and a teacher, reflecting back to you what you feel about yourself and illuminating areas of your life here you can learn and grow. They teach you about your boundary-setting, how assertive you are and, most important of all, how you feel about yourself. When you get to a point in your journey where you can see everyone, even people who have hurt you, as a gift to shine a light on those parts of yourself that need to be acknowledged and healed, you are truly falling in love with yourself. When you are able to forgive others and let go of feelings of pain and resentment, you are freeing your heart and mind from a heavy burden.

Remember, forgiving someone does not mean you are forgetting what they have done. You are simply refusing to allow the feelings you have about them to drag you down any more. And each time you forgive someone, you are also forgiving yourself for mistakes you may have made. Nobody is perfect.

Great expectations

One of the reasons relationships with sensitives turn sour or toxic is because sensitive people respond to energy. They give much of their time, attention and their own energy to their partner and expect a similar energetic response in return. What they don't appreciate is that other people may have a different way of expressing their love. For example, someone who approaches life more pragmatically may not be as great at listening or paying attention but will express their love through practical things, such as making sure all the bills are paid or the house is maintained. The sensitive may interpret this as not giving 100 percent.

For relationship success, sensitive people need to appreciate that what feels right for them in an intimate relationship may not feel right for someone else. They need to manage their expectations and understand that more grounded people have much of value to teach them, just as they have much to teach people who are less sensitive. They also need to understand that their intense and intimate approach to everyone can cause confusion.

Others may think that you want more intimacy than you are prepared to give because you were so attentive and absorbed when they first met you. From your perspective, however, long-term intimacy may not be what you want. You were simply giving someone your full attention at the time, because you don't do superficial chat. You may not necessarily want to follow through. Indeed, because you gave so much of yourself in your interaction, the chances are you now want plenty of time alone to recharge. The last thing you want is to meet the person again soon afterwards.

It's important, therefore, for sensitives to understand the impact of their gentle but intense attention on others. Sadly, lots of people don't have many others in their lives who are as attentive, so when you show you are listening carefully and with genuine interest, they are unlikely to want to let you go. You love making other people feel special, but this comes at a price. You need to find a way to be interested without giving other people the impression that you are a potential soulmate or lifelong friend, unless you have the intention of being that to them.

So, just as you need to manage your expectations about other people, you also need to find kind ways to help other people manage their expectations about you. The more you incorporate the sensitivity code strategies into your life, the easier it will become for you to express your feelings authentically and set boundaries in your relationships, whether intimate or more casual.

If disappointing people's expectations makes you feel fearful, remember to replace the word 'fearful' with 'excitement' or 'anticipation'. Think of your fear as excitement. You are feeling apprehensive because your authentic self is calling out to you to grow and evolve. Sometimes growth hurts. Your authentic self is highlighting what you need to do to improve the quality of your relationships, and the only way it can do that is by making you feel uncomfortable with the ones that aren't fulfilling you. Listen to what your authentic self is trying to teach you, work through the sensitivity code and be true to yourself.

Love lost

Losing someone you love, whether through death, divorce or a close relationship ending, is devastating for anyone, but for a sensitive person who feels things so deeply, it can lead to heartbreak and breakdown. It is not a myth – there is evidence[26] to suggest that people *can* die of a broken heart,[27] and in my opinion the chances are a great majority of those who do are highly sensitive. The agony of bereavement and heartache will be addressed in Chapter 7: The Spiritual Solution. It is during times of extreme emotional crisis that sensitive souls often find great strength through the search for a deeper meaning.

Sensitive parenting

If you decide you want to become a parent, the inevitable sensory overload that children bring into your life will make self-care vital. The additional coping strategies in Chapter 5 are particularly beneficial for sensitive parents.

When a sensitive person has a child, it can be an opportunity for them to revisit their own childhood. Instructions such as 'toughen up' and 'don't be a crybaby' or comments like 'you are just too sensitive for your own good' may have been thrown at you as a

26 Carey, I.M. *et al.* (2014) 'Increased risk of acute cardiovascular events after partner bereavement: A matched cohort study.' *JAMA Internal Medicine*, 174(4), 598–605.

27 https://www.bbc.co.uk/news/magazine-28756374

child, and you are certainly not going to talk to your own child in this way when they are feeling sensitive. In fact, you are likely to do the opposite. Just try not to go too far in the opposite direction.

Once again, I shall dip into my own life to illustrate the dangers of going too far in that opposite direction. I often felt harshly treated as a child because of my sensitive nature, and to compensate I overprotected my children with excessive nurturing, though I did not realise this was what I was doing at the time. I was determined to be 'mother of the year' and that they would not feel the same rejection I had experienced.

What I learned on my journey through parenthood is that you can love your children too much. They are both in their early twenties now and thankfully have survived my smothering, but looking back it could easily have gone the other way. It's a long story, but my son, who is highly sensitive, never settled into school. He was a clingy child. Dropping him off at nursery or school was pure torture. I remember days on end of sitting in the nursery car park, clutching my phone in my hand, so I could immediately swoop in if the nursery called and he needed me. I remember the nursery assistants peeling him off me, screaming, when I dropped him off. At junior school I was equally anxious and attentive, rushing in if the slightest thing upset him. He responded with constant stomach aches, headaches and illnesses, so that in the end he was off school more than he went in. Even though in his final year he was made head boy and was a popular child, it was always a struggle to settle him into the school routine.

My daughter, who is more grounded, coped better with nursery and school, but eventually separation anxiety swept over her too, so I decided to save everyone's tears and protect them from any chance of bullying by home-educating them both. For several years, starting when my son was 12 and my daughter 10, I put my writing aside to dedicate myself to educating them, with the help of my husband, who had recently retired. You could argue that it was a success, because at the age of 17 my son was offered a scholarship to the Royal College of Music to do a degree in performance there. My daughter went back to sixth form at the age of 16, and is now studying for her degree at the University of Cambridge. But all this success came at a price.

My son was extremely unhappy when he first started his degree, and went off the rails. It was a very tense time for my family. My overprotectiveness when he was growing up meant that he had not learned how to cope by himself when faced with life's challenges. Thankfully, he has now found his feet and his own voice and is flourishing. The relationship between us is loving and strong, but it nearly wasn't.

As for my daughter, home education gave her a maturity beyond her years, but she became withdrawn during her teenage years. Going back to sixth form was the saving of her. It took a while, and for a year we were barely speaking, but mercifully we are now back on track and our family is closer and more loving and appreciative of each other than ever.

The reason I'm sharing my parenting story is to highlight the dangers of the overprotectiveness than sensitive parents often manifest when they have children. At the time, I thought that I was simply being a loving parent, but I was not encouraging them to be self-sufficient. Of course, being over-involved in your child's life is better than neglecting them, but if you smother a child with love and protect them from every failure and disappointment, you rob them of the chance to learn about life for themselves, grow up healthily and find their own way.

I've finally learned that parenting is not about protecting your child from hurt, but more about gently letting go. The best gift any parent can give their child is to encourage them to trust themselves, and the only way a child can do that is to get out into the world and have adventures and make mistakes. I used to think it was cruel when I heard that mother birds simply kick their chicks out of the nest when they are ready to fly. My children sensed that I didn't trust them to fly and it took them longer to start trusting themselves. My smothering love could have cut me off from them forever. I thank my lucky stars that that never happened.

In short, the greatest challenge for sensitive parents is not that they can be overwhelmed by the noise and chaos children bring, but to trust that their children will be okay without their protection from the slings and arrows of life. It is tough for any parent to watch their child stumble and fall, face disappointment and rejection, but to take those transformative experiences away is detrimental to their emotional well-being. It is a cliché, but like many clichés it is the truth: the greatest love is the love that can let go when the time is right.

Sensitive children

Meditation, positivity and relaxation are highly recommended during pregnancy, whether a mother is sensitive or not. Neurological traits develop in the womb and pregnant women are encouraged to stay as calm as possible and flood their system with feel-good hormones. Research shows that if a mother is under stress or experiences trauma, it will impact the development of the foetus.[28]

If you recognise that your child is highly sensitive, use the tools and techniques in this book to encourage them to see their sensitivity as a gift. The earlier a sensitive person realises their own value, the more rewarding their life will be. When sensitive children are empowered, it is more likely that they will grow into confident adults, ready to dazzle the world with their creativity and heal the planet with their gentleness.

---

28 Coussons-Reid, M.E. (2013) 'Effects of prenatal stress on pregnancy and human development.' *Obstetric Medicine*, 6(2), 52–57.

Every time a sensitive person falls in love with themselves and makes their sensitivity work *for* rather than *against* them, the more peaceful the world will be. In many respects, sensitive people are eternal children, because a part of them stays forever young, filled with love, joy and wonder. They remind other people of what really matters in life and encourage them to pay attention to their own inner child. But without learning how to manage their sensitivity effectively, gentle people can be so easily damaged.

Walking alone

Sensitives certainly need regular time alone but they also need supportive people in their lives, as we all do. They are at their best when they are in love or giving others their full attention, yet every relationship they have, even painful or draining ones, teaches them something valuable – even if that is simply to learn the infinite power of saying no.

If you find, during the course of reading this book, that people do start dropping out of your life and your top-five list changes, remember that outgrowing people isn't just important, it is *necessary* for your personal growth. It is the clearest sign that you are evolving and transforming your gentleness into a strength. And it truly is better to be alone than with people who do not value or respect you.

Walking alone takes courage. But when you walk alone on a new path sooner or later you will encounter other courageous souls there who, like you, have made the empowering decision to be true to themselves.

A sensitive person can have the most fulfilling relationships both with people who are sensitive and less sensitive as long as they remember that there must always be a balance of give and take in every adult relationship. To really drive the point home, let's use breathing out as a metaphor for giving and breathing in as a metaphor for taking. Breathe out now. Fully empty your lungs and then pause for a second or two. In those seconds, notice how you feel and how essential it is to breathe in to correct the imbalance. Now that you have read this chapter, please don't get tangled up in draining relationships where you know you are not getting enough oxygen to thrive.

And, finally, please don't ever forget that although others can be our teachers and our mirrors, you also have much of great value to offer others. You can help those who are less compassionate and sensitive understand and appreciate the transformative power of empathy and gentleness. By simply being true to your sensitive heart you can become a healing light, inspiring everyone you encounter to make the world a kinder, more peaceful place.

Coming up...

Just as relationships can be messy, so can coping with the demands of everyday life. The next chapter addresses some of the most common things that overwhelm sensitive souls and suggests effective strategies for coping with them and finding inner peace in an insensitive world.

CHAPTER 5

Living in an Overwhelming World

Sometimes a sensitive person can find themselves bursting with feelings of love, compassion and happiness. This authentic joy surprises and delights them and is wonderful for others to witness. There may be a trigger for this positive energy shift, such as listening to beautiful music or watching a glorious sunset. But sometimes there is no trigger. You just feel unspeakably happy or grateful to be alive for no reason at all.

> Sometimes I am going about my day and life is very ordinary. Then, all of a sudden, a wave of joyful electricity blasts through me. I feel so incredibly happy and comforted. I can only compare the feeling to having a hot chocolate on a cold winter's day. Yes, it's that good.
>
> Trisha, 41

> Yesterday I was walking home. It was dark and the moon and stars were out in all their glory. The night sky was so very beautiful I had to stop and stare for a while, and as I did, everything in my life felt as it was meant to be. I felt like stardust.
>
> Ron, 22

I've never ever needed to get drunk or take drugs to get high. I can get high on life. Listening to music I love takes me to heaven, as does the beauty of nature.

Martha, 54

Those moments are sublime, a natural high. But the energy pendulum can swing the other way for sensitive souls, too. You may find yourself suddenly struck down by a tidal wave of sadness and dread. Sometimes there is an obvious reason – for example, I tend to feel wretched whenever I hear about any kind of cruelty to animals – but sometimes the sinking feeling can be utterly inexplicable.

I simply don't understand it, Theresa, but every time I get on the Tube, however hard I try to stay upbeat, by the time it gets to my stop I feel utterly miserable. Sometimes I'll have a headache, too, and I will sweat heavily even if it's a cold day. My Tube low has become so predictable and takes me so long to shake off that, to avoid ruining my day, I take the bus, even though it takes twice the time as the Tube.

Sally, 33

Some mornings I just feel rubbish. It's usually when the previous day has involved back-to-back meetings. Anyway, I wake up aching all over and feel utterly exhausted, even if I have had a very good night's sleep the night before. I usually feel better after I've had my breakfast and done some exercise, but I dread those low mornings.

Philip, 60

People who are prone to sensitivity have brains and nervous systems that can get more easily stimulated than others. When your brain and nervous system go into overdrive, it triggers the stress or so-called fight or flight response, which involves both physical and emotional responses. Your heart rate increases; you may also sweat, breathe faster, get an upset stomach and aches and pains, and feel anxious, fearful and sad. Over time, if you don't find ways to manage sensory overwhelm, it can lead to poor health, insomnia and depression. That's why it is crucial for sensitives to identify their overwhelm triggers and have protection strategies in place which they can immediately turn to and rely on whenever things feel too much.

This chapter reviews some of the most commonly reported overwhelm triggers for sensitive souls. It then offers a bespoke protection plan to help you manage overwhelm, whatever the trigger. It builds on the solid ground of increasing self-awareness and self-love that has been laid down in previous chapters.

Trigger: Me, myself and I

The advent of social media has contributed to a celebration of the material and superficial, but research[29] also indicates it may have contributed to a growth of a 'me first' or 'selfie' approach to life. What is considered acceptable behaviour today is something that sensitive souls often struggle to relate to. Perhaps you feel old-fashioned at times or that you belong to another era or planet because of the premium you place on kindness, politeness and respect for others.

29 McCain, J.L., & Campbell, W.K. (2018) 'Narcissism and social media use: A meta-analytic review.' *Psychology of Popular Media Culture*, 7(3), 308. Stuart, J., & Kurek, A. (2019) 'Looking hot in selfies: Narcissistic beginnings, aggressive outcomes?' *International Journal of Behavioral Development*, 43(6), 500–506.

One of my readers sent me this message. I'm including it here because it speaks volumes about the daily struggles faced by people who are sensitive in a selfie world.

> Yesterday I went out with a friend for lunch. The entire time she was texting. We would start a conversation but never really finish it because her phone would beep and then she'd answer it. This happened a dozen or so times. I had switched my phone off as I was looking forward to catching up with her. But I just sat there playing with the food on my plate while she smiled and texted. She did apologise every time it happened, but she didn't stop doing it. I understand she has a busy life, and that other people matter to her and she needs to be there for them. I also realise I shouldn't be selfish and demand all her attention. However, although this really wasn't a big deal, it truly made me feel unimportant. I didn't tell her any of this though, as I worried it would make me sound like a diva. I just smiled and said I was fine.
>
> Sophie, 37

Sensitive souls see beneath the surface of things and the masks others wear. Their intuition lies at the root of their compassion because what they see in others is the vulnerable inner child in need of love and validation. But their overflowing empathy and eagerness to make excuses for those who are devaluing them mean that they hand their power over to others.

It is often suggested that we live in a 'me first' generation. People are becoming less considerate of others and sensitive souls everywhere are feeling the pain. It isn't in their nature to treat other people with as little consideration as they so often experience. However, instead of pretending you aren't offended, that it doesn't matter or you are fine, it is very important that, as a sensitive soul, you find the courage to speak up for yourself.

Working through the sensitivity code every day will help you become more assertive. If anyone in your life makes you feel unworthy, speak up. And if that doesn't change the relationship dynamic, distance yourself. Remember, it is better to walk alone than with people who don't value you. You can start small. For example, if you hold a door open for a stranger and they walk through without saying thank you, smile and say 'thank you' silently to yourself. In many cases when I've done that, the person has responded with an apology for not noticing, but even if they ignore you, you have set the right tone. Then you can move on to more consequential things. For example, if a friend goes on their phone and starts texting whenever they meet up with you, simply say it would be better to reorganise your meeting when things are less busy for them and leave. Make your confidence felt.

Gentle people need to step out from the shadows and become more visible, because the world needs to see and hear them more than ever before. The social media generation, which places such a premium on money, success, looks and fame, isn't a very content one[30]. Just look at high-profile cases of rich and famous people who are depressed and unhappy, and increasing depression statistics[31] among teenagers.

Even though you may feel you are a minority, your gentle voice is one the world needs to hear, and has needed to hear since the beginning of time. Compassion, respect for others, love and kindness are what civilise humanity and make life worth living. If you speak up and politely point out to others when you feel

---

30 Hunt, M.G. *et al.* (2018) 'No more FOMO: Limiting social media decreases loneliness and depression.' *Journal of Social and Clinical Psychology,* 37(10), 751–768.

31 Twenge, J.M. *et al.* (2019) 'Age, period, and cohort trends in mood disorder indicators and suicide-related outcomes in a nationally representative dataset, 2005–2017.' *Journal of Abnormal Psychology, 128*(3), 185–199.

disrespected, this may fall on deaf ears, but it may actually help them to evolve. Not speaking up does them, as well as you, a disservice.

The sensitivity codes and the complementary protection plan in this chapter encourage you to speak out or make a change whenever you feel tempted to take a back seat in your own life. They will help balance the scales in your favour, given that you've spent a lifetime putting others first. It's simply impossible, given your sensitive soul, that you will tilt the scales from selflessness to selfishness and subscribe to the 'me first' mentality. And each time that you become more assertive, however insignificant, you offer others powerful food for thought.

Trigger: Health issues

Unsurprisingly, many sensitive people say they have rather delicate health. They are often the first to catch bugs and viruses doing the rounds. In addition, because their minds are so active, sensitives are prone to insomnia. And lack of sleep is known to lower immunity.[32]

> I don't sleep badly, I sleep terribly. Getting a good night's sleep has become my holy grail. Typically, I will fall asleep at around 11, but then I will wake up at one and then a few hours later. When I wake up my mind is racing and it takes ages to fall back asleep. I have had some of my best ideas in the early hours, but it makes me feel cranky in the morning. I also tend to need a nap in the late afternoon.
>
> Judy, 55

---

32 Besedovsky, L. *et al.* (2012) 'Sleep and immune function.' *Pflugers Archive*, 463(1), 121–137.

Sensitive souls who haven't found ways to manage their gentleness may resort to addictive behaviour, including eating disorders, comfort eating and substance abuse, to numb feelings of low self-worth and anxiety.

> When I leave the house I usually come back and check at least once that I have locked the door and unplugged the TV. Even though I 'know' really that I have locked the door and unplugged the TV, in my mind I imagine disaster scenarios. If my house exploded and anyone passing by was injured, I could not live with myself. I'm a compulsive checker.
>
> Heidi, 19

> In my twenties I was dangerously close to becoming anorexic. I think a part of me was so shy I literally wanted to be invisible. I was also an absolute workaholic, arriving before everyone else and frequently pulling all-nighters. I just wanted to make sure everything in my life was under control and I always did my very best. Letting people down was my ultimate nightmare. I'm gradually getting over that now and feeling calmer and more relaxed but I'm not there yet.
>
> Paula, 32

Fatigue and poor digestion due to high levels of anxiety are also common, as is a very low threshold for physical pain. Sensitives can often dread injections, the sight of blood and visits to the dentist. Last, but by no means least, some experts believe there may be a link between people who are prone to high anxiety and chronic health conditions.[33]

---

33 Segerstrom, S.C. *et al.* (2004) 'Psychological stress and the human immune system: A meta-analytic study of 30 years of inquiry.' *Psychological Bulletin*, 130(4), 601–630.

This all sounds alarming, but the intention is simply to alert you to the dangers of not taking special care of your health if you are feeling sensitive. There is a well-established connection between stress and poor health.[34] You probably know this stress and health interconnection to be true already. How many times have you got ill when you are feeling happy? Isn't it always more likely when you feel stressed and rundown? Equally, when you are suffering from poor health this saps your vitality and makes you less resilient to stress.

Daily self-care and doing everything you can to ensure you are as fit and healthy as possible is essential for everyone, but it is vital for people who are sensitive. There is a tendency for them to neglect their health and to push their bodies too hard, but some sensitives can swing the other way and become obsessive or paranoid about their health. If you fall into either category, the secret is to find a healthy balance and to diligently practise self-care. The sensitivity protection plan coming up will help you do just that.

Trigger: Clutter

Sensitive people often need minimalism to thrive. Clutter and chaos can totally stress them out. Empty spaces, tidiness and order soothe their souls.[35] Many sensitive souls could benefit from embracing the gentle art of decluttering.

> If my desk is untidy or my house cluttered, I can't concentrate on anything or anyone. I've been known to miss deadlines or postpone meetings because I have to clean the oven or vacuum the house first. I know it sounds nuts but it's just the way I am. To feel good and I need to know things are tidy and in order.
>
> Jonathon, 41

---

34 Hay, L. (2007) *You Can Heal Your Life*. Hay House.

35 www.highlysensitiverefuge.com/marie-kondo-highly-sensitive-people

Some people can live in chaos quite happily, but the soul of a sensitive person craves peace and harmony. An untidy, cluttered space can make them lose concentration, create anxiety, stunt creativity and trigger overwhelm. Focus and positivity won't be restored until order is.

Less truly is more for many sensitives. If clutter triggers feelings of overwhelm in you, the simple answer is to ensure your living and workspace is as tidy and as ordered as possible every day. If you have children and pets this isn't always going to be possible, but much of the clutter we accumulate is caused by disorganisation and lack of discipline. It takes just a few seconds to hang your clothes up or tidy things away or wipe something clean. Decluttering is a daily essential for sensitive people to thrive. That's why it's included in the protection plan later in this chapter.

Trigger: Cruelty

There is so much cruelty and pain in the world, and as a sensitive you are fully and painfully aware of that. If I even catch a glimpse of cruelty, I won't be able to sleep for a few weeks, because the image is burned into my mind. You may also find that if you witness any cruelty, particularly if it is directed towards helpless innocents with no ability to defend themselves, it can break your heart, your concentration and your capacity to feel joy for days and months on end. I often find myself bashing my head and keyboard in grief and frustration when I hear about cruelty and injustice of any kind in the news. I'm a spiritual writer and can't bear the fact that bad things happen to good people every single day.

Cruelty is a potent trigger for overwhelm. Often there is a powerful desire to do something, to help, save, donate or right wrongs. That's why many sensitive people are drawn to charity work or the caring professions. They will go to extreme lengths to strike out against injustice and cruelty in the world and to protect the environment, even overcoming their gentleness or hatred of crowded spaces to go on demonstrations or marches to promote a cause they believe in. There will be many occasions, though, when they realise that there is nothing they can do to help. This can cause feelings of despair and futility. What they may not realise is that there is one very positive thing they can do when they feel powerless, and that is to pray. Prayer, whether you are religious or not, is simply heartfelt communication between your inner wisdom and something higher or greater than yourself, and it can be incredibly healing.

Research isn't conclusive, and there may be no connection at all, but there is tentative evidence to suggest that people who are in hospital are more likely to recover if they are prayed for.[36] So, if you feel desperate to ease the suffering of others but can't help in a practical way, prayer is an option, and as you will see in the protection plan in this chapter, it doesn't have to be in the traditional sense of bended knees and palms together.

Trigger: Criticism

Nobody likes to be criticised, but sensitive people find criticism extremely hard to handle because they believe every word of it. Whether justified or unjustified, it can sometimes completely stop them in their tracks. Even if they get stacks of positive feedback from other people, they will likely focus on the one or two negative responses they receive.

This used to be the case for me. In the early days when my books started to appear online, there were the inevitable reviews. I would be on a high when the reviews were positive, but then the one- or no-star reviews came in. Instead of focusing on the

---

36 Andrade C. *et al.* (2009) 'Prayer and healing: a medical and scientific perspective on randomised trials.' *Indian Journal Psychiatry,* 51(4), 247–253.

glowing reviews, I could not take my mind off the negative ones. It was the same when I embraced social media. The online community is wonderful, but it can also be extremely cruel and negative. Reading the negativity felt like I was being hit over the head with a baseball bat.

It took me many years of pain to understand that whenever you have an opinion or put yourself on the line, there are always going to be people who respond positively, people who have no opinion about you at all and those who respond negatively. Successful people often take negative feedback on board and learn from it but they also focus on the people who understand them and don't waste energy trying to persuade those who will never be convinced. I wasted so much of my energy trying to help sceptics understand what I was aiming to do. I should have saved my energy for self-care, focused on who was reacting positively and not bothered with the rest.

It took me far too long to learn that you can't make other people like you, however hard you try or however kind you are. Unlocking the sensitivity code and practising the self-care strategies in the protection plan helped get me there. Now, whenever I get negative reviews and responses, I try to learn from them if I can. It is a positive thing to be challenged – there may be something I have missed or information that will help me evolve as a writer and as a person. If, however, the criticism is not constructive and simply unnecessarily cruel and hurtful, I send loving thoughts to whoever made it. I have come to understand that only hurt people intentionally hurt people.

Trigger: Betrayal

Being let down or betrayed by people they trusted or cared about can hit sensitive people harder than most. Because they care so deeply about the well-being of others and have personal integrity, when they encounter people with dubious moral codes, they are blindsided. Their first response is to find excuses for that person, and if one can't be found, their next response is incomprehension followed by devastation. Truth and integrity are sacred for them.

If you do find yourself constantly being let down or your trust being abused, this is a sign that you are not setting clear boundaries in your relationships and are trusting others before they have proven to you that they can be trusted. Remember the advice in Chapter 4 to trust a person by what they do and not by what they say. Until you learn that, life will continue to challenge you and you will keep meeting people who have dubious morals or who struggle to tell the truth. It's a lesson I am still learning to this day.

Trigger: Goodbyes

Saying goodbye to anyone or anything is an intensely bitter and difficult experience for sensitives. They are highly nostalgic and loyal to friends, institutions and even things. The previous chapter discussed sensitive relationships in depth, so I won't repeat what was said there except to say that sensitives do need to learn to say goodbye to people in their life who they have outgrown or who are not respecting them. They need to stop fearing endings and see them instead as new beginnings.

The great majority of our relationships and friendships are not meant to be for life but for a season. You'll know that already from your school or college days. On the last day of term, everybody promises to keep in touch forever, but a year down the line, everybody has moved on. Although friendships can be lifelong, we tend to spend most of our time with people who are treading a similar path, and your colleagues likely become more significant in your life than your school or university friends. Then, if you have children, you spend time with other parents, and so on as you move through life. The partner or friend for life can only happen if that partner or friend gives you space to grow separately from them and you return the favour. In most cases, the people in our lives frequently change as we evolve and expand our horizons. Of course, the most painful goodbye we ever have to say is the final one, when people die. More about how to navigate the trauma of bereavement in the next chapter.

It's not just people that sensitives need to get used to saying goodbye to. They can become hoarders, unable to get rid of objects and clutter because of the memories associated with them. They can also stick with beliefs, societies, groups, institutions and things they have outgrown for the same reason. I will step in here to give an example from my own life.

My readers will know that for the last 20 years I have stood by my trusty angeltalk710@aol.com email for readers to send their stories. Over the years my publishers and countless advisers have urged me to upgrade to Gmail or Outlook.com or something more trendy-sounding. I know I probably should, as AOL has had its issues, but when it comes to making that change, something inside me winces. I remember how excited I was to receive my first email. I remember the thousands of incredible messages I have received from readers all over the world and how they have made me gasp, cry and laugh – sometimes at the same time. It's as if that email address has taken on a life of its own, and even though it's not the trendiest email to have, I continue to use it to this day.

Of course, there's a place for nostalgia, and I'm not advocating that you throw everything in your life that isn't shiny and new out of the window. All I am saying is that it is important to be aware of the tendency you may have to hang on to things that you have outgrown. Your reasons for not letting go may be entirely sentimental, and that's fine – as long as holding on to them doesn't drag you down. You need to weigh up the pros and cons of looking back to the past to see if it is creating a present that is fulfilling you. If it isn't, then it's time to say goodbye to the past with gratitude and look to the future with excitement.

Trigger: Animal cruelty

On my son's tenth birthday we had an exciting day planned for him to go paintballing with a few of his friends, followed by a trip to the cinema and a restaurant. However, the day didn't happen as planned, because in the morning my son found a tiny chick in the garden, gasping for air. We spent the entire morning setting up a cardboard box and feeding the chick using a thimble. As lunchtime approached, the chick was not responsive. I phoned my local vet who suggested the RSPCA (the Royal Society for the Prevention of Cruelty to Animals), but as it was a Sunday their nearest animal rescue centre that was open was 30 miles away. I told my son I would take the bird there and he should go to his party, but he made the decision to cancel the party. The only thing that mattered to both of us was the tiny chick.

As we drove to the RSCPA, we speculated on what kind of bird we had found. My son was convinced it was a hawk because of its majestic beak. He was heartbroken to have to give it away as he wanted to nurture it himself at home, and that's what we would have done if the bird had been thriving under our care. When we got to the centre, the wonderful staff there took the cardboard box from my son's hands and said we could call in a few days to find out how the bird was.

We did call a few days later and were thrilled to hear that the bird was thriving. It wasn't a hawk, it was a pigeon, but we didn't care. We went to visit that pigeon and watched it fly away when a staff member released it a few weeks later.

Only the sensitive people reading this will not burst out laughing. It was just a pigeon, for goodness' sake! But many sensitive people care deeply about animals, however commonplace. There hasn't been any research but I'm guessing that a high percentage of people who are vegetarian or vegan or opposed to animal experimentation are sensitive. There is something about an animal's blind trust, vulnerability and inability to communicate with words that speaks directly to our hearts. Perhaps some of us see our own vulnerability in them.

I also wouldn't be surprised if a high percentage of sensitive people own pets. For some, the relationship they have with their pets is so strong that, if push came to shove, a few might admit they prefer the company of animals to humans, or that they feel a deeper connection to them. The unconditional love and uncritical companionship pets can give is incredibly healing. My little dog, Arnie, is the love of my life. If I am going anywhere my first thought is often who will look after Arnie. When I get home at the end of the day, nothing brings me more happiness than seeing him bound towards the door. And I'm not ashamed to say that some of the best conversations I have ever had have been with Arnie!

Sometimes the love I feel for my dogs and my cats is so intense that I just want to cry. I used to think feeling this way was strange, but sensitive souls and animal lovers will know what I am talking about. Pet bereavement hits sensitive souls particularly hard. It goes without saying that any kind of cruelty towards animals sends me into a cold sweat and triggers many a sleepless night. One of the reasons I stayed away from my social media, even though I had built it up to over 100,000 followers, was a fear of what images of animal cruelty I might see on my news feed. One image in particular kept me offline for two years.

Closely associated with a love for animals is a love of nature, and the protection plan will encourage you to continue to indulge your love for both. Spending time with pets and in nature offers you a safe place, a refuge when life overwhelms.

Trigger: Social media

It's not just animal cruelty images on social media that are distressing; there is a whole world of pain, brutality and X-rated content online that is wildly disturbing. Even if you adjust all your controls to try and filter it out, it is impossible to avoid coming into contact with it. On top of that, social media is an arena of judgement, negative criticism, fake ideas and lies that can make your head spin.

If looking through your newsfeed, seeing your friends' selfies and updates and feeling anxious about how your own posts will be received trigger overwhelm, it's time to do a social media detox. Whether you are sensitive or not, research has shown that people who spend time on social media tend to feel more depressed afterwards than before.[37] Social media is meant to connect us, and when used wisely it can be a brilliant force for good. But if you find yourself getting depressed after using social media, chances are you are seeking affirmation there. Remember the first rule of the sensitivity code: don't seek validation outside yourself, seek it within.

Trigger: Movies and TV

If you are like many sensitive people, you will typically have a movie or TV show that made a deep and lasting impact because it terrified or upset you so much. For me that movie was *The Exorcist*, but I can name countless others. I have left the cinema shaking with fear or feelings of revulsion, with the images of horror, cruelty or violence so imprinted on my mind that they flash into my thoughts for weeks, months or even years afterwards.

---

37 Hunt, M.G. *et al.* (2018) 'No more FOMO: Limiting social media decreases loneliness and depression.' *Journal of Social and Clinical Psychology*, 37(10), 751–768.

Sam sent me this enlightening read. It highlights perfectly how sensitive souls process movies and TV.

I grew up in the seventies and eighties. Television was a huge part of my life. It dominated my family and home life. I had no idea that I was highly sensitive back then but I did realise that I was responding to the images on screen in a very different way to my brother and sister. I didn't just watch the shows and movies. I lived them. If a character was being chased or attacked, I would feel a knot in my stomach. If a character was happy my heart felt light. My parents told me that sometimes I would actually get up and physically role play what was happening on screen. It was all totally unconscious. I wasn't aware I was doing it. I just lost myself in the drama. It was extremely hard for me to distinguish what was real from what was not real. I remember one time, I must have been about six, that I actually tried to crawl behind the television to see if the characters on the screen lived there.

When I got a little older and started to watch the news and more adult-themed TV there was a downside to all my TV watching. When I watched episodes of *Star Trek* or *Doctor Who* with scary aliens or monsters, I would cover my eyes with a cushion or hide behind the sofa in fear. Even though I knew it was acting and not real as soon as the credits rolled, I was right there in the screen, feeling everything intensely. My siblings felt scared too but were not immersed in the emotions as I was and were able to shake off their fear when the show was over. I didn't have that ability to leave the memory behind.

Ghost stories, in particular, would haunt me for days, weeks, sometimes months afterwards. I would relive the scene over and over again in my mind and not be able to sleep for fear I would see a 'real' ghost. There was one movie I saw, I can't recall the title, but I do recall that the lead character only saw ghosts whenever he looked in the mirror. You guessed it. I was terrified to look in a mirror for a very long while afterwards. I also had a super tough time processing the news. News reports from areas of natural disaster or famine or war would cripple me. I would have to leave the room. I could feel the suffering with every part of me.

Decades later I don't look behind the TV or hide behind the sofa any more but I haven't changed that much either. I still can't watch suffering on news reports and I have to closely monitor everything I expose myself to on screen and online on my newsfeed. Disney movies make me cry as much as they always did. The death of the particular character in Harry Potter, for instance, left me utterly inconsolable. Tears flooded down my cheeks. I have to ask everyone to check the content of a movie before I pay money for a ticket because if an appealing character dies or there is any violence or horror, I simply can't cope with it. I have to leave the cinema. I love gaming but it's frustrating for me as I can't play any games that are uber violent and many of the best games fall into that category these days. But even the ones I do play it is simply impossible for me to sit down with the controls. My adrenaline kicks in and I completely immerse myself in the experience. Even though I'm in my fifties now, I'm right there inside the game, just as I was right there inside the TV when I was a kid.

Sam, 40

Other movies may not have such a shocking effect, but they can still make you feel deeply emotional. The memories of Bambi's mother being shot in the Disney movie *Bambi* or Jack's death in *Titanic* still make me choke up to this day. There is something about cinema, in particular, that makes me emotional, and I have even found myself crying during the adverts. If you recognise yourself here, the solution is simple: do your homework before going to the cinema and check if there are any disturbing images in the film you are going to see. If there are and you know you won't be able to stomach them, don't let family and friends pressure you into going.

Sensitive people don't observe, they feel – and when the film is over, they can't shake off emotions and move on as quickly as others do. The images linger on and disrupt peace of mind and the chance of a good night's sleep. We can't shut off our feelings or be exposed to images of cruelty and regard them as entertainment. Such things cause us emotional pain.

Unlocking the sensitivity code will help you find the courage to assert yourself and let others know what you can and cannot tolerate. It is a very positive thing that there are people, like you, who aren't becoming desensitised to cruelty and violence. Without sensitive people, imagine how harsh the world would be. But, of course, you can't protect yourself against everything, so if you do witness something that triggers you, you can leave the cinema or switch off the TV. Or if that isn't possible, acknowledge your upset, and when it replays in your mind afterwards, close your eyes and visualise a different and happier story.

Trigger: Noise

Sensitive people are often hypersensitive to noise[38], and from childhood are able to pick up sounds that others miss. This is a wonderful ability and bodes well for budding musicians, but it

---

38 https://hsperson.com/noise

can cause problems if you live or work with noisy people or are exposed to noise.

> For the final two years of my degree I shared a house with three other people. It was the wrong decision because I need peace and quiet to study, and after a few weeks they started to get really loud. I couldn't study or get a good night's sleep because they played music or had constant loud parties and arguments all day long and late into the night. I tried to tell them but they just ignored me and said I was being a bore. The noise didn't seem to bother them. I didn't want to cause tension, so I tried to find ways around it. I couldn't work in the library because my computer was in my room, so I started to work really odd hours, in the small hours of the morning, simply to get some peace and quiet. It got to the point where I couldn't be in the house during the day because the noise was driving me insane.
>
> Charlie, 28

Research has shown that noise pollution can damage hearing and disturb peace of mind, so if you know that you are highly sensitive to noise, you need to protect your ears and your sanity. Invest in some comfortable earplugs if you live with a partner who snores. Wear them during the day if you need to reduce your exposure to noise. Avoid loud concerts and nightclubs. If you have a friend who shouts rather than talks, you must either accept this about them or ask them to tone it down for you. Find ways to minimise noise pollution. Don't try to soldier on and pretend you are okay. Your hearing is sensitive and you need to protect yourself.

Trigger: Crowds

Just as loud noises can trigger overwhelm, so can large crowds. Many sensitive people have an instinctive fear of crowds. I like to think this is their inner wisdom speaking to them, reminding them that they need to stop trying to please the crowd or other people. Do everything you can to avoid being in crowds, but if you find yourself unexpectedly in a large group of people, practise the relaxation and visualisation techniques coming up and tell yourself that soon this crowd will pass.

It's the same if you feel your personal space is invaded by people getting too close, for example when they talk to you or (and this one always gets to me) if you are sitting in a restaurant or café and someone sits right next to you, even though there are empty seats elsewhere. You always have the choice to move or step back, but if that isn't possible – if, for example, you are on a crowded train or Tube – be sure to put your protective bubble on. It is worth noting that during times of enforced isolation sensitive souls are unlikely to mourn the loss of social gatherings and many are likely to adjust far better than those who are less sensitive.

Trigger: Food

You may find that you are highly sensitive to caffeine, dairy, alcohol, wheat or gluten, or you may be food intolerant in some way. You need to become a detective and find out what you physically can't tolerate. If you have to eliminate certain foods or drinks from your diet because you know they are triggers, go ahead and do so. If someone serves you food you know you can't tolerate, tell them politely that it doesn't agree with you – don't just eat it for fear of causing a fuss. That strategy will almost certainly backfire, as you won't be able to hide the physical and emotional effects. Gently assert yourself, but don't go overboard. Remember, balance in all things is key.

Triggers: Multitasking and being watched

Sensitive people thrive when they can fully invest their energy into one thing or one person at a time. They don't usually excel when required to multitask or when they are surrounded by distractions. Indeed, when too many demands are placed on them at the same time, this can cause mental confusion and feelings of overwhelm.

Everyone leads busy lives today, and people who multitask tend to be celebrated. I'm going to turn things around now and champion the power of focus. Great things are typically not achieved by multitaskers but by people who have focus and who refuse to be distracted. Take Usain Bolt, for example, who is widely considered to be the greatest sprinter in the world. Just look at the concentration on his face when he is sprinting. Everything else is shut out and there is just one focus.

If you know that multitasking is going to trigger you, the best advice is to plan your schedule the night before to avoid the chances of multitasking happening. Of course, sometimes it won't be possible for you to pour all your focus into one task or person at a time – for example, if you need to make a call and are walking your dog or holding a baby – but the more you work through the sensitivity code and protection plan below, the easier and more natural it will become to find inner peace and focus during stressful times.

The same advice applies if your trigger is being watched or observed. You may never be someone who enjoys public speaking, but life is about evolving. You can learn to manage your thoughts and emotions to give you the ability to step outside yourself for a much-needed sense of perspective whenever panic strikes.

Your highly sensitive protection plan

Although there are certain triggers that typically cause sensitive souls to feel overwhelmed – above, I have listed some of the most common that people who are sensitive have written to me about – never forget that you are unique and may have your own unique triggers. It may help to keep a mood diary to see if you can identify your triggers. This is a diary where you record the events in your day, the people you have met, the things you have done and so on, but you also record your moods and emotions at the beginning and end of the day as well as during. Over time you can then refer to your mood diary to see if a pattern emerges and if you can identify any triggers.

Obviously, the common-sense advice is to try to avoid a situation that you know will surely overwhelm you. However, if avoidance isn't possible for family, work or other reasons, then manage the situation by applying the protection plan strategies below.

Bear in mind that sometimes overwhelm doesn't appear to have a trigger. It just strikes. As soon as you feel yourself at risk from overstimulation or overwhelm, the following practices and tools can help you cope.

Breathe deeply

If you start to feel anxious, the first step is to pay attention to your breathing. It is likely to have become quick and shallow or erratic. Breathe in through your nose as slowly and as deeply as you can. Then immediately breathe out, expelling all the air from your lungs. Repeat until you feel calmer.

Use the protective bubble

When you are with people or in an environment that feels draining and you start to feel overstimulated, the next step is to try the protective bubble technique, where you visualise a bubble of light all around you that stops anything overwhelming from reaching you.

Detach yourself

You need to master the art of emotional detachment, which is the ability to step outside yourself to observe what you are feeling, thinking, saying and doing. From that position of emotional detachment, and with an understanding that everything you feel is your choice, you can *choose* to remain calm.

The next time you feel anxiety, for whatever reason, take some time out, acknowledge (out loud if you can) that you are feeling on edge and then detach yourself. Step outside your thoughts and feelings. Watch what is happening within and around you as if you were a witness.

Taking a step back when you are a sensitive person who gives their whole heart is a challenge. But letting people or things dictate your energy suggests that you are relying on externals you can't control to make you feel happy. You aren't paying enough attention to Sensitivity Code 1, which explains that happiness can only be found from within. You are also losing sight of the sensitivity code mantra that you are *not* your thoughts and your feelings do not control you. In this case, you are *not* your feeling of overwhelm.

Removing attachment to other people and situations doesn't mean you don't feel engaged and passionate any more. You can still feel passionate whenever you choose to, but the difference is that you no longer allow other people or things to define you or rely on them to complete you. You understand that when you feel overwhelmed it is because you have lost perspective and the ability to step outside yourself and observe what is happening to you.

Unlocking the sensitivity code is all about helping you master the subtle art of detachment. I truly believe a key life lesson for sensitives is to take things less personally and to stop expecting other people to behave in a certain way. What people do or say is never about you but about them. Detach and let go of expectations. Other people are not going to behave as you want or expect them to, and they also cannot make you feel a certain way. They can't heal you either. Healing is your inside job.

Just say Om

Contrary to what you may believe, meditation is not complicated or time-consuming to learn. It is a very simple way to connect to your inner calm and a particularly helpful strategy to employ whenever you feel overwhelmed.

There are so many different ways to meditate and I encourage you to do some research and discover what you enjoy the most. You may want to download a meditation app or you may simply wish to take some time to sit in silence and observe your thoughts. You can focus on your breathing when you meditate or you can focus your attention gently on the clouds, the stars or a tree.

You may also like to use the power of sound and chant the word 'calm' or 'peace', or another word associated with calm, such as 'Om', over and over again. Chanting is known to encourage relaxation, ease stress and boost well-being. Research suggests that the sound vibration you create when you chant really can make you feel happier, more energised and focused.[39]

Chanting, like prayer, is associated with religion, but just as you don't need to be religious to pray, you don't need to be religious to enjoy the benefits of chanting. If chanting makes you feel odd, remind yourself that it is not much different to humming, which many people do to help them relax and concentrate.

---

39 Kalyani, B.G. *et al.* (2011) 'Neurohemodynamic correlates of "OM" chanting: A pilot functional magnetic resonance imaging study.' *International Journal of Yoga*, 4(1), 3–6.

Each morning, begin your day with a few moments of chanting. As you chant, believe you are attracting peace and calm into your life. If you are new to chanting you may want to start with the most famous and ancient mantra of them all – Om, which is pronounced 'aum'. This ancient sound vibration feels so calming and exhilarating. You can then chant mantras or words that mean something important to you. It doesn't really matter what you chant or how you chant, as long as you use chanting to infuse your life with joy.

If you don't wish to chant, you may prefer to listen to some calming music, with or without headphones, depending on what you are doing. My personal favourite to immerse myself in completely when I feel stressed is the first movement of Beethoven's *Moonlight Sonata* or Debussy's *Clair de Lune*. Music calms and heals my soul every time.

Drink water

In recent years I've got into the habit of bringing a bottle of water everywhere with me and when I feel overwhelmed I make a point of sitting down somewhere quiet and drinking it mindfully. It's a strategy that calms me and it might just help calm you too. Most of us really underestimate just how essential staying hydrated is for optimum well-being. Contrary to what you may think, if you wait until you are thirsty to drink, you are already severely dehydrated.

Brain and nervous system function are connected with hydration because your brain is approximately 85 percent water.[40] Around eight glasses of water a day is recommended, but everyone is different. If you regularly sip water throughout the day you will be drinking the right amount.

---

40 Ganio, M.S. *et al.* (2011) 'Mild dehydration impairs cognitive performance and mood in men.' *British Journal of Nutrition*, 106(10), 1535–1543.

Take supplements

A healthy diet, regular exercise and fresh air, as well as getting enough sleep, will boost your health and well-being so that you are less vulnerable when overwhelm strikes. As far as diet is concerned, a balanced diet, rich in fruits, vegetables and wholegrains, will help protect your nervous system. There are, however, some supplements that might particularly benefit people who are sensitive, but do be aware that supplements can have side effects. Consult your doctor if you are thinking of taking them.

- **Vitamin B12** (found in dairy, eggs, tuna and fortified cereals) is especially good for strong nerves, but as the B vitamins work best in synergy, you may want to start taking a vitamin B complex supplement every day.
- **Magnesium** (found in nuts, seeds and green leafy vegetables) plays a key role in the function of the brain and the nervous system. If your levels are low you may be more susceptible to overwhelm, so you may wish to consider a magnesium supplement.
- **Fish oil** is a rich source of essential fatty acids, which can help improve mood. Taking a fish oil supplement may help you feel calmer and more balanced. For vegan sources of those mood-boosting essential fatty acids, try flaxseed or soy oil or fish oil supplement alternatives.
- **Digestive enzymes** may be helpful if your digestion suffers when you are under stress.
- **Chamomile and passionflower** are herbal remedies that can encourage a good night's sleep if racing thoughts keep you awake at night.
- **CoQ10** is a replenishing antioxidant that can help fight fatigue caused by overwhelm.

If you have any food intolerances, consult your doctor or a nutritionist for diet recommendations, and if you know you are highly sensitive to caffeine, sugar, wheat, gluten, dairy or alcohol, then avoid them.

Tidy up

You may have heard of Marie Kondo's book *The Life-Changing Magic of Tidying*, or the Netflix show *Tidying Up with Marie Kondo*. If you haven't, the message is simple: do some tidying up every day.

Regular decluttering is incredibly beneficial for everyone[41] and particularly for sensitives who are triggered by clutter.[42] The moment you start tidying up your living spaces, ridding yourself of mess and material clutter, is the moment you introduce a much-needed sense of calm and order.

If you haven't been diligent for a while and are surrounded by clutter, but don't feel you have to do a time-consuming purge or spring-clean right away, it can feel overwhelming. Start small, with the simple act of making sure your bag and your pockets are emptied out and tidied every day. Let this small act inspire you to tackle other small tidying tasks during the day, such as organising a sock drawer, cleaning your bathroom sink, donating items you no longer need to charity or just washing up your mug or cup rather than leaving it on your desk or in the sink. It doesn't have to be anything major. Small acts of tidiness every day can help you minimise clutter and experience the life-changing magic of living clutter-free.

---

41 https://www.sharecare.com/health/stress-reduction/article/the-health-benefits-of-decluttering

42 McMains, S. *et al.* (2011) 'Interactions of top-down and bottom-up mechanisms in human visual cortex.' *Journal of Neuroscience*, 31(2), 587–597.

Take time out

Regular time out isn't a waste of time. It is absolutely essential for sensitive souls who need alone time to recalibrate and recharge as much as they need the air they breathe. Don't be tempted to cut out your downtime under any circumstances. You will regret it. Be sure to incorporate regular quiet periods in your day when you can daydream or do something that replenishes you, such as going for a brisk walk, reading or listening to music.

One of the most popular and calming ways for sensitive people to take time out is to enjoy a warm bath, preferably with relaxing and beautifully scented bubble bath or Epsom salts, which are great for easing stress. Many people who are empathetic people have written to me to say they have a deep affinity for water – in spirituality, water symbolises emotions – and they are never more content than when soaking for a long time in a luxurious bath or hot tub. It's not just a bath for them, it's a *power* bath.

Schedule your day

Sensitive people are likely to suffer from overwhelm when they are forced to multitask or are up against tight deadlines. Knowing your vulnerability in these situations, make scheduling the day ahead a nightly ritual. Every evening, portion out your time for the next day, so that you can focus on one thing at a time. Then stick to your timetable the next day.

Successful people plan ahead or set out a framework for what they want to achieve each day.[43] Planning your day by writing a timetable the night before will help you avoid overwhelm. You will wake up knowing what you want to achieve that day and how you are going to achieve it.

---

43 www.success.com/5-daily-habits-of-highly-successful-people

While it is important to wind down at the end of the day, if you take some time to create a framework for the next day, you will be surprised by how much your productivity soars.

This evening, and every evening from now on, spend a few minutes planning the next day. Begin by laying out the clothes you will wear. Then sit down and give your undivided attention to planning ahead. Schedule your day as precisely as you can or write a to-do list which you will systematically work through. It doesn't matter how you plan, just remove some of the guesswork that is likely to trigger overwhelm. Be aware that the first few hours when you get up are often crucial for setting the tone of the day, so try to do your essential tasks then.

Unplug yourself

These days, most of us have our eyes glued to screens much of the time. Texts, emails, messages and updates bombard us, and the more sensitive you are, the more overwhelming the invasion can be. The digital world is addictive and we fear we will miss out if we aren't constantly scrolling. In fact, the opposite is true, as there is a well-established link between depression and too much screen time and social media use.[44]

If you are worried about missing out, don't. Relying on technology every moment of the day is unhealthy, and taking regular time away from screens and social media will reduce your risk of overwhelm, boost your mood and help you focus and sleep better. Very little that we consider urgent actually is. The goings-on or opinions of others won't change or improve your life, but giving yourself regular time to unplug and put the focus firmly back on yourself will.

Make a commitment to yourself to have at least one hour in the morning and evening away from technology, especially your

44 Shakya, H.B. *et al.* (2017) 'Association of Facebook use with compromised well-being: A longitudinal study.' *American Journal of Epidemiology*, 185(3), 203–211.

smartphone. Unplugging for the first hour of your day is recommended because what you do then will set the tone for the rest of the day – if you reach for your phone first thing, the message you send the universe at the start of the day is that the needs and opinions of others matter more than your own. You may also want to set a regular time in the evening, say seven p.m., when you switch off your phone and let everyone know that you can't be reached. Whatever time of day you choose, stick to it and make your unplugging time sacred for you. It doesn't matter what you do in that hour either – you may decide to meditate, exercise, walk, tidy up, write in your journal, sing or dance. As long as it doesn't involve a phone or a screen of any kind, it's perfect.

And when you have made regular unplugging a daily ritual, you may want to take stock of your phone use, and delete apps and social media that are constantly sending you unnecessary alerts and notifications. Given what research suggests about the link between using social media and depression, it makes sense to limit the amount of time you spend on it – or, better still, make a decision to leave it altogether. This will also limit your exposure to potentially upsetting images.

The world won't stop if you aren't posting updates in your accounts. Give it a try and see how much better you feel when you stop letting your phone control your life. You may even want to join the growing movement of people who are ditching their smartphones and (shock horror!) simply using call-and-text-only phones.

Get your nature fix

Science is now clearly indicating what we intuitively know: a daily dose of nature is good for everyone.[45] It is especially beneficial for

---

45 Boubekri, M. *et al.* (2014) 'Impact of windows and daylight exposure on overall health and sleep quality of office workers: A case-control pilot study.' *Journal of Clinical Sleep Medicine*, 10(6), 603–611.

sensitive souls. A cluster of recent studies have linked depression, stress, poor concentration, insomnia, fatigue, anxiety and poor health to disconnection from nature. Nothing helps boost well-being more than a simple walk in the woods. There is no better way for a sensitive soul to find much-needed inner calm than to see green.

If your life and work is indoor-focused, and you don't live near the countryside or a park, this isn't an excuse. There are ways you can incorporate a return to nature into your daily routine. It can be something as simple as leaning against a tree, buying a potted plant or just getting more fresh air.

As a society we are increasingly dislocated from the outdoors due to our reliance on technology and urban-based living, but the fastest way to boost mood and focus is to step outside. A walk in the woods or the park is obviously ideal, but if that's not possible just head outdoors and seek out the nearest green space or garden. If going outdoors isn't an option, open your window, drink in the fresh air and watch the clouds drift or the stars sparkle. The more time you spend in nature or green spaces, and the more you make nature a part of your daily life, the happier you will feel. And if you can, try a little barefoot walking on mud or grass. Studies show that direct physical contact with the earth through 'earthing' (the term for barefoot walking) can boost mood and health.[46]

Spending time in nature also ensures you get plenty of natural light. We need the vitamin D from natural light to strengthen bones, balance hormones and boost energy. Regular exposure to natural light is especially important if you suffer from insomnia. If you have trouble sleeping, be sure to make seeking at least 15 minutes in natural light every morning a daily ritual, as the amount of natural light you are exposed to during the day can inform your internal clock when it is time to sleep.

46 Chevalier, G. *et al.* (2012) 'Earthing: Health implications of reconnecting the human body to the earth's surface electrons.' *Journal of Environmental Public Health*, 12, 291541.

Spend time with animals

If you own a pet you will know that animals can offer your sensitive heart remarkable unconditional love and comfort, both when times are good and when times are bad. If you don't own a pet, you might want to consider adopting one, but if you don't want to or can't own a pet, you can still learn a great deal from animals. They set us an example of the power of living in the present and savouring each moment.

Volunteer to help

If you are triggered by an injustice or an issue that makes you feel powerless, such as animal cruelty or climate change, there are ways you can do something to help. For example, you can volunteer to help in an animal shelter or plant a tree. If you love walking beside the sea but the sight of plastic on the sand makes you angry, join a community litter collection service.

Find ways to channel your frustration productively. If you feel that your contribution is pointless because the world is unjust, think of this famous story about the stranded starfish and the boy throwing them back in the sea. When told by someone that there were thousands of starfish stranded along every shore, so what he was doing wasn't making a difference, the boy picked up another starfish, and before throwing it back into the sea said, 'Well, it will make a difference to this one.'

The sensitivity code has focused on the importance of self-care. But sensitive souls often find that combining self-care *with* helping others is the perfect combination to ease their anxiety. Once you have paid attention to your own needs, see if you can help someone. It will temporarily distract you from your anxiety and calm you with a helper's high. Knowing you are making a difference to the lives of others will immediately make you feel better. Just be sure though, given your susceptibility to always putting the needs of others before your own, that helping others is always combined with helping yourself.

Say a little prayer

The sensitivity code has already touched on the power of prayer and you may wish to say a little prayer whenever you feel anxious or overwhelmed. You can pray to a spiritual or religious figure, or to an angel, fairy or spirit, or you can address your higher self. It doesn't matter who you choose to pray to, simply asking for peace and protection in the eye of a storm can be effective. You don't have to pray in the formal way on bended knee either – you can pray anytime, anywhere, silently with your thoughts.

As well as helping protect your energy, prayer can also be a healing force. Try this experiment: the next time someone doesn't respect you or hurts or betrays you, send that person silent healing with your thoughts instead of frustration or anger. You'll be surprised how this counterintuitive response can help heal you, and perhaps even them.

Other ways

Below are some other tried-and-tested protective strategies you can use whenever your feel overwhelmed or at risk of being overwhelmed. Experiment with them or do some research and find out what works best for you, as the sensitive souls in the following stories did.

> I use a technique known as the emotional freedom technique (EFT), in which you tap pressure points on your face or various other parts of your body with your fingers. I don't really understand how it works, but it does make me feel calmer. I tap several times under my nose, above my top

lip, and say out loud what the problem is. For example, 'too much to do' or 'feeling like I will mess up', and I keep doing that until the intensity has gone. And then I repeat the tapping and tell myself I'll be okay, using phrases like, 'I don't need to be concerned', or 'I can do this'.

Michael, 44

Walking my dog is my energy protection. I start the walk feeling stressed and always feel so centred when I return. I always meet other dog walkers when I'm out and I could be wrong but I think it is the same for them. I love my dog, and when I walk him, it's like taking my heart for a walk to give it much-needed fresh air and perspective. Think about that the next time you see dog walkers. They are taking their hearts out for a walk.

Mike, 29

The most effective strategy for me when I feel over-whelmed and I don't feel I want to talk to my friends is to go somewhere I can be alone and have a really good cry. It's cathartic. Tears seem to wash things away and give me a better perspective.

Carla, 17

The best therapy for me is spending time with my beloved cat. She is so calming. When I am not at home and can't stroke her to calm myself down, I have a rose quartz crystal that I take with me everywhere. It's my good luck charm. I think crystals have healing power. Rose quartz is the crystal for self-love and that is the area of my life I most need to work on. When I feel stressed I hold it in my palm and place it close to my heart.

Nicola, 60

I visualise the colour purple swirling all around me from top to toe when I get overwhelmed. It refreshes my spirit and makes me feel better. Then, if I still haven't shaken off negative feelings, I like to burn sage or lavender incense for their cleansing properties.

Rebecca, 47

Whatever path you choose to help you navigate overwhelming or uncertain times, you can't go wrong if you ensure it includes the four 'M's: Mindfulness (feeling grateful for the present moment and focusing on what you have, not on what you don't), Movement (getting lots of movement to boost your health, mood, energy and immunity), Mastery (reminding yourself of challenges you have overcome in the past as well as finding something you can master. It doesn't matter what it is, find something you love to do and become good at it) and Meaning (finding a deeper meaning to things or looking beneath the surface, see Chapter 7).

Don't stop believing

Remember, you absorb the emotions of others and drink in atmospheres. If you don't protect yourself, you will feel drained. All the strategies here are protective and offer different ways to manage and protect your energy rather than repress or deny it. You will have noticed that none of the strategies ask you to change your sensitive personality, but simply to manage it in order to protect yourself from overwhelm.

Your gentleness is not a flaw. Quite the opposite. Your gentleness is *who you are*. It defines you and is your greatest strength. You should not try to change your authentic self. Don't stop being the sensitive soul you were born to be. You should continue to feel deeply and approach the world around you with empathy, kindness, love and compassion, especially when others don't reflect that gentleness back to you. Even if you do feel exhausted and unappreciated, don't be tempted to switch off or deny your sensitivity. It will only make matters worse for you and for the world. Without sensitive people like you, the world would be such a cruel and dark place.

Don't ever forget that the sensitive personality trait you are blessed with in abundance has not faded away. Scientists may beg to differ but if sensitive traits were weaknesses or irrelevant to our survival as a species over the course of time we would perhaps have lost our connection with them. I believe that your instinctive empathy, intuition and gentleness have survived for millennia for a reason. And that reason is to bring much-needed connection, healing and wholeness into our lives.

Coming up...

Sensitives often fail to recognise the remarkable potential of two of their defining personality traits, empathy and intuition. Chapter 6 discusses the power of empathy and intuition to heal yourself and the world and explores everyday ways to transform them into extraordinary superpowers.

CHAPTER 6

Your Sensitive Superpowers

All the personality traits that sensitive people possess have the potential to be truly extraordinary. Take your natural inclination to be kind, for example. The remarkable thing about kindness is that not only does it have feel-good endorphin benefits for both you and the receiver, but there is another third-party effect.

Research has shown that whenever a third-party witnesses or hears about an act of kindness, it inspires them to be kinder.[47] If you've ever seen someone give up their seat on a train or on the Tube for a pregnant woman or an elderly person, you will be aware of this third-party effect. Seeing kindness happen is motivating. In other words, kindness is contagious. Every kind act you perform has a ripple-like potential to encourage others to reach out with similar acts of kindness, changing the world for the better, one kind act at a time.

This chapter isn't going to focus on your instinct to be kind though, or the power of your creativity and gentleness to light up the world. It is going to focus on the two traits sensitive people most often fail to understand or see the potential of. The reason for this is that they are both traits that are invisible. Others aren't aware that you have them.

---

47 www.scientificamerican.com/article/kindness-contagion

Your empathy

The first invisible superpower is empathy, the ability to look outside yourself and sense or feel what others are feeling. Empathy and compassion are closely related, but compassion is doing or saying something to help, comfort or ease the pain of others, whereas empathy is an inner sensing or understanding of another person's situation or point of view. It is simply being present and 'seeing' another person's heart and state of mind. Many sensitive people are acutely aware of their empathy, but have no idea how to process it or understand its potential.

> If someone starts to tell me about their problems, I imagine I am in their shoes. I feel their anguish. It's tough for me because I don't know what to do with all these feelings that aren't my own. I'm like that with strangers, too. I'm the one at a party who always gets stuck listening to someone nobody else will talk to. I feel their loneliness.
>
> Len, 20

Studies show that empathy has transformative benefits.[48] It can foster a sense of connection with others that can be healing for both parties. We all crave to be heard and understood by the people in our lives. Sometimes we don't want someone to do anything but simply listen to us and be present. Not surprisingly, empathy is essential for positive and loving relationships. It can help resolve conflict, and it is a source of creativity and innovation because it encourages understanding of the needs and opinions of others. It invites an open-minded approach to others and makes us more likely to be compassionate.

---

48 Riess, H. (2017) 'The Science of Empathy.' *Journal of Patient Experience*, 4(2), 74–77.

Although the part of the brain associated with empathy is more responsive in sensitives, everyone has the innate ability to be empathetic. Our brains have mirror neurons[49] which help us learn by imitation and by so doing help us better understand the actions, movements and emotional states of others. In other words, your mirror neurons give you the ability to sense or feel what someone else is feeling, which is the definition of empathy. For example, it's your mirror neurons that are at work when you witness someone falling over and you flinch momentarily because you 'feel' their pain and embarrassment.

For sensitives, seeing the world from another person's perspective doesn't just happen when watching movies or sports teams, it happens in all their interactions. Every day we step into the shoes of others, both those we are intimate with and those we barely know, such as the barista who makes our coffee or the person who delivers the post. Being empathetic has its downsides. It can be a draining experience if you don't learn to set boundaries. The sensitivity code encourages you to set clear boundaries and practise protection techniques, so you don't attach yourself to what is not yours. But setting boundaries does not mean you should shut off or repress your empathy. Far from it. Empathy is what connects the world. It is what reminds us of our similarities rather than our differences. It is what we need more of, not less, especially in the increasingly divided world we live in today.

I see you

Empathy helps us understand how other people feel, think and act. It is hardwired into everyone's DNA, but is more developed in sensitive people than others. Because it is invisible and doesn't

---

49 Iacoboni, M. (2009) 'Imitation, empathy, and mirror neurons.' *Annual Review of Psychology*, 60, 653–670.

involve doing anything except simply feeling what someone else is feeling, it is easily dismissed as having no real value. But empathy has incredible value. It can connect and heal the world.

Although the world has never been more connected due to virtual and on-screen connections, people are feeling increasingly anxious, alone, unhappy and isolated with actual human contact decreasing. The more anxious and unhappy a person is, the less empathetic they become. Technology, the breakdown of families and the rise of intolerance and nationalism play a large part in this disconnection, but whatever the reason, empathy is dying and narcissism is relentlessly on the rise. Sensitive people who manifest empathy excess rather than deficit have the power to reverse this troublesome trend.

In Zulu, the word for 'hello' is *sawubona*, which means 'I see you'. Sensitive people 'see' other people. They are present for them. There is nothing more validating than being noticed. People post on social media because of their urgent need to be 'seen', but online validation and connection is an illusion because it does not involve genuine human interaction.

Sensitives show that it is human nature to interact with other people. When we convey to someone else that we 'see' or witness their feelings, we convey that we understand where they are coming from, even if we don't necessarily agree with them, and the effect can be truly healing and empowering. It makes someone who may previously have felt invisible or alone, or that they must suffer in silence, feel seen. There is no greater gift you can give to another person than making them feel seen.

Your empathy, therefore, is far more than a sensitive personality trait. It is a remarkable and much-needed gift from you to the world. Learn to manage it but never ever try to repress or deny it. To risk repeating myself, the world needs more empathy, not less.

Your intuition

Like empathy, intuition is an invisible gift, but whereas empathy is looking outside of yourself and sensing what others are feeling, intuition is looking within yourself and following your gut instinct.

Your intuition is an untapped source of higher wisdom. It is that still, calm voice inside you that knows what is right for you before you do. It is an awareness of thoughts, images, feelings and physical sensations that can provide you with meaningful information about your past, present and future. Some even consider intuition to be a form of sixth sense or ESP (extrasensory perception). Many highly successful people credit their intuition as a powerful ingredient in their success. They typically describe it as an inner voice, some kind of knowledge within them that has guided or inspired their work. 'I just knew' or 'I trusted my gut instinct' are phrases they often use.

To summarise, intuition is your connection to the wise part of you – an unconscious reasoning that urges you to say or do something when you don't really have any idea why or how you know it. It is a knowing without knowing that can provide you with valuable insights about yourself, others, situations and life. It is not a moral compass or authority on what is absolutely right or wrong for everyone. But it does provide a sense of what is right for you and what is in your best interests. It is informed by – but also beyond – logic and experience and is, quite simply, an amazing source of wisdom and potential. It is your highest self, the best possible you.

Sensitives are highly intuitive souls, but all too often they find it hard to identify, connect to and trust their inner wisdom.

> If only I had listened to my instinct. The first time I met my ex, a feeling of dread came over me. I remember

looking at him and seeing his face morph into something unpleasant. It was just a fleeting impression and that moment passed. I told myself I was being paranoid. I wasn't. He cheated on me on the night we got engaged.

Tania, 34

Anxiety and low self-esteem can lead to loss of concentration and poor decision-making. Intuition typically strikes when we are in a calm and relaxed state of mind. That's why we often have our eureka ideas not when we try to force them through brainstorming, but after a good night's sleep, or when we are distracted by something that puts us in a semi-meditative state that doesn't require much thought, such as walking, showering or travelling.

Unlocking the sensitivity code is therefore perfect for igniting the raw power of your intuition, because it is all about increasing your self-awareness and reducing anxiety about your sensitivity. The more you unlock the sensitivity code and step into your own power, the calmer and more confident – and therefore more intuitive – you will become.

Meeting your best self

Intuition has often been called the ultimate path to happiness and the highest form of intelligence. It goes hand in hand with the superpower that is your empathy, because the more empathetic you are, the more intuitive you are likely to be.

There is very real science to show that intuition or sixth sense is not New Age nonsense.[50] Its benefits have been studied and validated. Over the years I have interviewed and worked with some of the world-leading scientists and neuroscientists who are

---

50 www.psychologicalscience.org/news/minds-business/intuition-its-more-than-a-feeling.html

researching the power of what is invisible and the inner world.[51] I have made it my mission to help spread the word about these pioneering scientists who are acknowledging that what is felt, sensed or unseen is as valid a topic for scientific research as what is external or seen. (If you want to check out my interviews with these scientists, please visit the resources section.)

Both scientists and psychologists agree that the more you follow the voice of your intuition, the better life choices you will make and the happier you are likely to be. Connecting to your intuition is the fast track to a fulfilling life. It is also a way to evolve into the best possible version of yourself. Each day you tune into your inner wisdom takes you one step closer to fulfilling your potential.

But how do you know when your intuition is speaking to you and what is the best way to boost it?

It takes time and practice to recognise when your intuition is speaking to you. I therefore encourage you to keep a record of your intuitive hunches so that you can see when you are correct and when you are not, and identify a pattern. There is nothing like proof to give you a confidence boost.

But how can you tell when your intuition is speaking? Intuition is that calm and gentle voice within you. If your inner voices are harsh, negative, erratic and judgemental, this is not your intuition but anxiety speaking. Your intuition will always speak to you in a focused way that empowers you. The feedback will be constructive and goal-orientated.

Another way to identify intuition is that it tends to surprise you – the hunch comes out of nowhere. It is also likely to be limited in words and will simply encourage you to take action. The voices of fear do the opposite. They chatter loudly and argue like crazy.

---

51 Cheung, T. and Mossbridge, J. (2018) *The Premonition Code*. Watkins Media.
See also: www.noetic.org/Theresa-Cheung
See also: www.theresacheung.com/my-podcast

Your thoughts sweep you off your feet and you think of nothing else, trapped in endless discussions and indecision. Intuition, on the other hand, speaks through certainty. There will be no spin, just peace. Intuition will always have your best interests at heart and will never belittle you or make you feel 'less than'. It also won't steer you away from your values. It will feel right in every way.

Trust in me

Learning to recognise and then trust and develop your intuition is a book in itself (yes, your intuition is correct, I've written a book about how to tune into it too) but for now, here are some sure-fire ways to ignite your intuition:

- Pay attention to unusual bodily signals, such as a raised heart rate, sweaty palms, butterflies in the stomach, dry mouth, unexplained aches and pains or tingles. Obviously, all these signals could also be cause for medical concern if they linger or are repeated so seek medical advice. The bodily signals I'm referring to here are fleeting and temporary ones. Research has shown that the first place your intuition is likely to speak to you is through your body, with physical sensations.[52]
- Recall and pay attention to the intuitive messages sent to you in the symbolic language of your dreams, or as I like to call them, your night visions.
- Learn to meditate, because in the meditative state you don't try to force or control things, you free your unconscious wisdom. Regular moments of peace and calm can also reduce your levels of anxiety, which is the enemy of your intuition.

52 www.sciencedaily.com/releases/2012/10/121022145342.htm

- Notice your feelings. Most of us focus on our thoughts during the day, but you need to notice both your thoughts and your feelings, as your feelings play a big part in the way intuition communicates to you.

In a nutshell, the best way to ignite your intuition and meet your higher self or inner wisdom is to unlock the 12 sensitivity codes in Chapter 3 every single day. These strategies are designed to help you understand yourself better and give you the self-belief you need to confidently and calmly connect to the wise voice of your intuition.

Born gifted

Over the years I have been sent countless stories from sensitive people about their hunches, or their ability to sense what is unseen or impossible to know. Here's an example:

It's taken me decades to come to terms with my sensitivity, and there have been bouts of low self-esteem, dipping into depression, over the years. Today I like to think of myself as an empath or highly intuitive and sensitive person.

From a young age I have been able to sense what others are thinking and feeling. There's a positive side to all this, as it means I can reach out to those I care about and offer to be there if they need me at exactly the right time. Lots of my friends tell me I'm psychic because of this. There's also a negative side. If someone I am close to is going through a rough time, I literally feel it. This is where things get complicated. Sometimes it is hard for me to know where I end and they begin. I feel the pain of those I love.

To give an example from many, on more than one occasion I have woken up in the middle of the night with a feeling of inexplicable dread. In June last year I woke up and thought of my aunt. I'm close to my aunt, as my mother suffered from poor health when I was at school. My aunt would often be there to take care of me when my mother couldn't. I noticed the time when I woke and it was 2.22 a.m. I made myself a cup of tea and sent healing thoughts to my aunt. I made a mental note to call her in the morning, as it had been a few months since we had been in touch. We had spent the morning together shopping. I noticed she got out of breath a lot but otherwise she seemed perfectly happy and content.

The next day I got a phone call from my mother. My aunt had suffered a stroke and died overnight in hospital. There had been attempts to save her but to no avail. The recorded time of death was two thirty.

Sasha, 57

This isn't the place or the book to debate whether psychic abilities are real, but unsurprisingly, psychics, healers, channelers and mediums typically possess highly developed powers of empathy and intuition. Recent research into psychics and healers has indicated that there is a strong genetic component and the 'gift' is often handed down from generation to generation.[53] I believe this 'gift' to comprise highly sensitive personality traits more than anything else. I'm not claiming here that all sensitives have psychic or X-Men-style powers. All I am saying is that because of their highly developed empathy and intuition, the potential to develop their sixth sense and become 'psychic' is there.

How a person responds to the challenges and blessings of their sensitive feelings and traits will always be a choice. You may not choose to investigate your psychic potential, but hopefully this

---

53 www.windbridge.org

chapter will have helped you recognise and celebrate the vast potential of your empathy and intuition. They are supernormal powers that no one can see, but they can help heal both you and the world. They can also silently guide and inspire you on your lifelong search for deeper meaning, which is what the final chapter in this book is all about.

Coming up...

Chapter 7 explores the search for deeper meaning that defines the lives of many sensitives. They have to feel passionate about what they do and will often regard their work as a vocation rather than a job. Unsurprisingly, given their instinct to seek deeper meaning, many find themselves drawn to spirituality. The soul is the place where they discover their deepest fulfilment and joy.

CHAPTER 7

The Spiritual Solution

Since as early as I can remember I have wanted my life to have meaning. I'm not alone, as many sensitives I have spoken to over the years feel exactly the same about their lives. They genuinely want to make a difference in the world. Many hope their careers or the work they do can give them that sense of meaning. If their work does not fulfil them or offer them a rewarding opportunity to serve or help others, they will spend a lot of time trying to figure out what exactly it is that they are 'meant' or destined to do with their lives. Feeling passionate about their work matters to them.

Finding your purpose

Sensitives need to feel that their lives have purpose, and the first and most obvious way they seek to find that purpose is through their career. They may devote a lot of thought and energy to trying to find the work they were 'born' to do. They may change jobs time and time again or return to study or education to help them find their vocation.

If you recognise yourself in this and feel your current job or occupation isn't suited to you, rather than hating it or feeling you are wasting your time, it might help to focus on what your current job is teaching you or providing for you. If it doesn't fulfil you but you need the money, think of this job as a means to an end, providing you with the financial means to support your search for fulfilment. If you can reframe all your work choices as necessary steps towards your life goals or where you want to be, then no job you ever do in your life will be a waste of time. There is something to be gained or learned from every job you do, however menial or trivial you may think it to be at the time.

Stressful and busy workplaces that require constant networking, presentations, meetings, deadlines and travel don't tend to suit sensitive souls, but their love of education and learning and wish to help others will see many of them gravitate towards professions such as lecturing, teaching, medicine, writing, counselling and law. The arts, religion and spirituality also appeal to them greatly.

Given their thoughtful natures, practical jobs or jobs such as banking, where the focus is entirely on making money, may sometimes feel stressful for them. But, having said that, practical tasks may be therapeutic, helping them stay grounded, and business-focused jobs can give them the financial means to live life on their own terms. Whatever work they do, there is always a danger for sensitive souls to lose their head in the clouds. Ironically, jobs that require little thought may be good news for them, because mindless work has a meditative effect, freeing their creativity for bigger ideas. In short, sensitives can thrive in any career as long as they understand what their strengths are and don't fall into the sensitivity traps of low self-esteem, people-pleasing and the perfectionist's fear of failing (and therefore never trying).

Even though there is something to be gained from any kind of work, however menial, many sensitives do want to find what they feel is their vocation or higher calling. In their search for this calling they encounter many contradictions within themselves.

See if the following contradictions resonate with you.

- You likely want to help or serve others but feel drained when people take advantage of you.

- You have the self-discipline to work long and hard, making you an asset to any organisation or business, but your whole-hearted approach puts you at risk of burning out.
- You love time alone and need peace in your workspace, but you also need to feel that you are making a difference to others.
- Money is not your first priority, but you want to ensure you have enough to take care of yourself and provide for the people you love.
- You want to save the planet but fear your gentle voice isn't assertive enough to be heard.
- You have great business ideas but struggle to set boundaries with colleagues and get the recognition you deserve.
- You love to be part of a team but can't handle workplace politics, and your values prohibit you from exhibiting the ruthless killer instinct often required to rise to the top.
- You want to achieve so much with your life but don't have the confidence to ask for advice or help.

With so many conflicting inner voices talking to you at the same time, it can be hard to know what you really want your life to be all about.

Your vocation equation

If you are struggling to find what your purpose is, this vocation equation, inspired by a concept in Japanese culture called *ikigai*, may offer some inspiration.

In Japanese culture the secret to fulfilment lies in finding your reason or your meaning in life – your *ikigai*.[54] You may find this

---

54 Mogi, K. (2017) *The Little Book of Ikigai: The Secret Japanese Way to Live a Happy and Long Life.* Quercus.

in the work you do, but you are more likely to discover it in your approach to life. Instead of encouraging you to slow down to smell the roses and consider your options, your *ikigai* stirs you to actively get out there and find your meaning in every aspect of your life, not just work. The emphasis this concept places on being proactive and taking action can be particularly helpful for sensitives, who can become so lost in thought and a fear of making the wrong decision that they become indecisive.

Research indicates that the Japanese may be right, and being fully engaged in whatever you are doing, and finding fulfilment and meaning in that, brings more satisfaction than money.[55]

To incorporate the ikigai spirit into your life, focus your thoughts on these three questions:

- What do I love?
- What am I good at?
- What does the world need?

If you aren't sure what will fulfil you, think about what you loved to do when you were a child or what you would do with your life if money was no problem. What makes you feel truly alive? What absorbs your attention so fully that you lose track of time? Think also about what you are good at, or what you could be good at if you studied. Once you identify what you love to do and what you are likely to be good at, discover how this can be used to serve or help others.

To ease yourself into the *ikigai* mindset, start small. For example, in answer to the first question, ensure that during your day you seek out three small joys that light up your day and make you feel alive. Write those joys down and give thanks for them. In answer to the second question, write down three things you are good at and actively seek out ways to utilise those skills during the day. In answer to the third question, you can discover what the world needs by connecting actively to it and being present in the here and now. Make a point of noticing what is going on in your environment and appreciating its sensory beauty mindfully. Hear what other people are saying. Be curious. Be proactive. Constantly look for ways in which you can help others and make the world a better place.

Through small but positive changes, you can reshape your brain, boost your mood, shift your mindset and train yourself to live a life of actively seeking your purpose or *ikigai*. Research shows the average lifespan of a Japanese person exceeds other countries.[56] Their diet, which is rich in grain dishes, vegetables, fish, meat and fresh rather than processed food, is a big reason for their high life expectancy, but perhaps their tireless search for *ikigai* is part of the story, too?

If you feel despondent or repeatedly wonder what the meaning of your life is, the first step is to consider whether you could be depressed, in which case you need to seek professional medical help. If this is not the case you may also want to consider whether you are being called by your higher self to find your purpose. Remember how the sensitivity code has encouraged you to reframe fear, anxiety, despondency or feeling like an imposter as positive signs that you are out of your comfort zone and that you are therefore growing and evolving. *Ikigai* sounds mysterious and complicated, but it truly isn't. It is simply describing the need within all of us to always seek purpose in life. It is a metaphor for spiritual awakening or the search for deeper meaning.

---

56 www.independent.co.uk/life-style/health-and-families/health-news/high-
   life-expectancy-in-japan-partly-down-to-diet-carbohydrates-vegetables-fruit-
   fish-meat-a6956011.html

Finding deeper meaning

The final chapter of this book ends where Chapter 1 began – with a journey of self-discovery. In the spirit of the immortal words of T. S. Eliot, 'and the end of all our exploring will be to arrive where we started and know the place the first time'. I hope that this book is helping you to understand the infinite strength and potential of your authentic self as never before.

Finding out that you are a sensitive person and that personality traits you once considered to be weaknesses or flaws are in fact strengths is a spiritual awakening, because it encourages you to be authentic and true to yourself. As previously mentioned, in ancient times sensitives were the shamans, healers, visionaries, artists and oracles of their people, and offering guidance, wisdom, inspiration and healing were their vocations. Today, sensitive traits are no longer revered in the same way, but these spiritual leanings remain hardwired. It is their calling. Rediscovering their inner shaman, healer, visionary and artist is the path for many sensitives to find their true meaning. They can do that through the work they choose to do or through their approach to life.

The deepest fulfilment for sensitives is therefore not necessarily found in work but in spiritual development. Of course, not all sensitives will identify with spirituality but I am inclined to believe a high proportion do because of all the thousands of messages I have received over the years from sensitive souls. The great majority of those messages focus on spiritual experiences and a belief that there is more to this life than meets the eye. Dr Elaine Aron's pioneering research[57] into high sensitivity also confirms that sensitive people typically have a deep connection or fascination with the spirit world and are highly receptive to spiritual experiences and beliefs. They may not always be able to articulate that a spiritual force is at work in their lives, but they

---

57 Aron, E. (1999) *The Highly Sensitive Person*. Thorsons. Chapter 10.

strongly believe this. Indeed, for the highly sensitive it would not be a stretch to conclude that developing spiritually is essential for their fulfilment and happiness.

It is important to point out that although religion is a spiritual path that brings fulfilment to some people, religion and spirituality are not the same thing. Most sensitives struggle with rules and regulations and tend to follow the spiritual rather than the religious path. But what is the spiritual path?

The spiritual solution

If you haven't already guessed, the sensitivity code strategies offered in Chapter 3 draw heavily on a spiritual perspective that we are spiritual beings having a human experience rather than human beings having a spiritual experience. In other words, there is an eternal, non-physical part of us that sees the bigger picture or higher meaning of our lives and which, depending on your beliefs, may survive bodily death. That eternal part of us is our soul or spirit, the higher power or force that exists within everyone and everything, connecting us all through the power of love.

If you are sensitive and have ever wanted to find out the meaning of your life and what you are supposed to be doing with it, the spiritual approach can offer you the answer. You have likely always felt that there is a deeper meaning or that there is something higher or greater to your life. Spirituality shows you that answers can't be found in material things, or through your thoughts and emotions, because they are the human part of you, which is defined by your upbringing, your schooling, your career, your relationships, your bank balance and other worldly things. You can only find answers about your life purpose through stepping outside of your human experience and connecting with the spark of eternal spirit or love within you.

You can call this eternal spark your inner wisdom, higher self, soul, spirit, energy, force or God, but however you define it, this is the part of you that sees the bigger picture or higher meaning of your life and can guide you away from identifying yourself with the material and superficial towards what really matters. Throughout your life you will often experience a tussle or struggle between what your human self, or ego, needs and what your spiritual self wants. Many times, your human self speaks loudly and more aggressively. It speaks from a position of fear and it is the voice that makes you lose confidence and belief in yourself and seek external validation from other people and things. But even during the darkest and most confusing times, it is still possible to connect to the gentle, loving voice of your spirit, which knows that the only validation you need comes from within.

Spiritual calling cards

In subtle ways, your spirit speaks to you primarily through the invisible voices of your intuition and empathy, which as the previous chapter explained, are sensitive superpowers. There are other subtle ways your spirit can speak to you though, which you may not have been fully aware of before.

Spirit can speak to you through the symbolic messages of your dreams. Every night when you fall asleep, your inner wisdom is sending you guidance, comfort, warnings and answers to questions, all of which can help you change your life for the better. Think of your dreams as your inner therapist – and much cheaper than a real one.

The problem is that many people don't recall their dreams or, if they do remember them, they tend to dismiss them as meaningless because dreams are often so hard to understand. Sensitive souls would benefit from dream recall as research indicates that people who recall their dreams feel calmer and healthier.[58] But if you don't recall your dreams, this doesn't mean you are not dreaming. It just means that you are not remembering them.

---

58 https://greatergood.berkeley.edu/article/item/why_your_brain_needs_to_dream

To encourage dream recall, every night before you go to sleep leave a notepad and pen beside your bed. When you wake up the next morning, write down what comes to mind. The reason most of us forget our dreams is because they fade from our mind because we don't take note of them immediately. If you still can't recall anything, write down in your notepad that you can't remember the dreams. The simple act of doing that will signal to your dreaming mind that you *are* paying attention and this may help you to improve your dream recall. In my experience, and from what I have noticed helping people understand their dreams, the more you think or talk about your dreams, or the possibility of having them, the more likely you are to succeed in recalling them.

To help you understand the surreal messages of your dreams, simply write down what you dreamed about in the present tense and don't try to make it logical. Then, later in the day, reread your dream diary and see if any associations come to mind. You may want to use a dream dictionary to help unlock the meaning of your dream symbols, but do remember that every symbol in your dream is unique to you and will have your own personal associations attached. For example, if you love dogs, dreaming about them is comforting for you, but this is the opposite for someone who fears dogs.

Be aware, too, that every person or thing in your dreams represents something about you. Your dreams paint a picture of your state of mind, so don't take your dreams literally. For example, if you dream you are having an affair with a colleague, this does not mean you fancy that person, but that they represent an aspect of your personality you need to greater incorporate in your life or come to terms with. If you dream about a loved one dying, this does not literally mean they will die, it means that your loved one represents an aspect of yourself that you have outgrown. Something in your life is ending, but with every ending there comes a new beginning.

Dream interpretation is a book in itself, and I've written the bestselling *The Dream Dictionary A–Z* about this, which you can find out about in the resources. I encourage all sensitive souls to study their dreams carefully and become their own dream interpreter. Listen to the messages your dreaming mind is sending you.

Coincidences are another way that spirit can speak to you. Pay attention to synchronicity or the feeling that you are in the right place at the right time. And don't stop there. Notice gentle signs from the universe everywhere you go. Seek meaning or the extraordinary in the ordinary. The romantic poet Blake famously saw the world in a grain of sand, so why not see it in a white feather, a rainbow, a sunset, a passing cloud? Why not hear it in a gentle breeze, a bird's song, the voices of loved ones or anything that inspires and comforts you? Why not see the universe as it truly is: a place of infinite possibilities and unexpected wonder?

Taking the spiritual path

Don't think that the spiritual approach to life means your life should be peaceful and happy, or that you have failed if you aren't in a constant state of bliss. This couldn't be further from the truth. You will continue to face struggles because, as previously explained, we grow through our challenges. The purpose of our life is to learn from the mistakes we make and from the challenges we encounter – and sometimes growth hurts. But what may be different for you, if you walk the spiritual path, is that you will have a much-needed change of perspective that can help you understand and cope better.

It is during dark times that we grow the most, and the spiritual approach can help us deal with challenging times. It shows us that there can be a higher meaning behind all the confusion and suffering. We have to trust in the eternal power of love. Perhaps this metaphor will help explain the unexplainable. The underside of a tapestry is all knots and loose ends. This is how we view our lives from a material perspective; nothing appears to make sense. But when you turn over the tapestry, or shift your perspective to a spiritual one, you see a beautiful picture in which everything makes sense.

There is no denying that life can be cruel and unfair. Why bad things happen to good people is the unanswered question that sensitive people lie awake at night wondering about. Again, the spiritual approach can offer comfort and peace. Suffering is the darkness before the dawn, the light at the end of the tunnel. It is the pain of childbirth. The spiritual approach encourages us to keep on asking the eternal 'why' questions even though we know there can be no definitive answer. Indeed, it suggests that the power is in the asking. For example, every time we question the reason for suffering and injustice, we bring a welcome dose of empathy and compassion into the world. Imagine if we knew the answer to why there is suffering. We would not reach out to others or care as much. We would become indifferent to the suffering of others and that would be a terrible thing.

The spiritual perspective reminds us that because our spirit or authentic self is separate from our body, mind and emotions, we always have a *choice* about what we choose to say, do, feel and think. We can choose to detach ourselves from material things. Spirituality also focuses on the similarities we have with other people, rather than the differences. Spirit is the eternal force of love, kindness and compassion in all of us, which unites and reminds us that we are all connected.

Beyond grief

Perhaps the most transformative effect the spiritual approach to life can have is in helping sensitive souls to cope better with the bitterest pill we must all swallow at some time in our life – bereavement. Grief can be overwhelming for anyone, but for sensitive souls who feel emotions so acutely, it can be nothing short of devasting. And it's not only bereavement that can trigger an intense and long period of grieving, because sensitives are hit harder than most by loss of any kind, be that heartbreak, divorce or redundancy.

As a sensitive person, my first encounter with the sharp pain of grief was in my twenties when my mother died. I was not prepared for the tsunami of feelings that hit and plunged me into full-blown depression.

Depression feels like collapsing into a tunnel of darkness in excruciating slow motion. For me, at the time, there was no way forward or backwards and the only thing that existed in my life was darkness. I had no energy. Some days even turning my head from side to side hurt. Life had no light, not even any shades of grey; only blackness, fear, hopelessness and suffocation in a dark, lightless existence. Even my face began to tell the story of my grief. I didn't have the energy to use facial muscles. Whenever I glanced in the mirror, I looked dull and blank, with unfocused and vacant eyes.

In short, depression hit me in a relentless and vampiric way. For sensitive people who are so emotional, no longer feeling anything at all equates with becoming the living dead. Reluctant to trouble others, all too often we don't reach out for help or support. We put on a brave face even though we are dying inside.

Sensitives typically grieve more intensely and for far longer than other people. Understanding the grief process can help them navigate the inevitable stages of denial, anger, bargaining, despair and eventual acceptance that they need to move through in order to come to terms with personal loss. The spiritual perspective gives them the inner courage to see that there can be light at the end of the tunnel. The body is transient but spirit is eternal. Death can therefore be viewed as an opportunity to enter into a new relationship in spirit. Death ends a life but not a relationship.

Indeed, for many sensitives, coming to terms with the loss of a loved one is the catalyst for spiritual awakening. Before that awakening can happen though, you need to grieve fully and let go of your attachment to the past, so you can allow the love you gave the person who has died to return to you and make you whole again. If you are grieving the loss of a loved one, I recommend watching the Oscar-winning Disney movie *Up*. It is an animation, but it contains great wisdom for people of any age going through the trauma of bereavement. Warning: Like most heartfelt Disney movies, *Up* will likely make a sensitive person cry.

Spiritual awakening

Grief, however, isn't the only catalyst for spiritual awakening in sensitives. There are many other catalysts.

Of course, there are some extremely rare people who seem to have been awakened by the miracle of their birth; people who see beyond the here and now and spend their lives in an enlightened state. But for the great majority of others, myself included, that isn't the case. What happens as we grow up is that the voices of fear and doubt creep in, destroying the peace and contentment that is our birthright. When fear rules our hearts, there isn't room for peace, so we need something to happen in our lives for us to 'wake up' and recognise the need to turn inward and re-evaluate our priorities. Sometimes this intervention has to be pretty dramatic to ensure we take notice!

Reviewing the thousands of messages and letters I have received over the decades I've been writing about spiritual growth, and from my own personal experience, I have identified some of the most common signs or experiences that indicate spiritual awakening.

- **Dissatisfaction**. Perhaps the most common sign – and often the first. You start asking questions and begin to doubt everything you thought to be true or real about yourself and your life. During this time, you may try to seek answers in philosophies, religions or the New Age movement, but sooner or later you discover that the road to awakening has to be found within. It can only be found by asking yourself who you are.

- **Confusion**. Perhaps you thought you knew yourself well, but then suddenly find yourself doing something out of character, surprising yourself and others. You may suddenly feel compelled to seek adventure in your life, do wild or completely different things or mix with people you normally would not.

- **Loss**. You may see no way forward for yourself after a major loss, failure, rejection or setback in your life.. Sometimes you just need to accept that what you are experiencing is necessary for your soul to evolve.

- **Grief**. As mentioned above, the death of a loved one is the most painful loss of all. Your life is turned upside down, but bereavement is often the catalyst for seeking deeper meaning in your life.

- **Brush with death**. Perhaps you have had a brush with death, have been in poor health or have suddenly been reminded of your mortality. This can be a powerful trigger for spiritual awakening.

- **Curiosity**. You may suddenly feel urgently compelled to read about the experiences of others and how they found their meaning.

- **Depression or addiction**. Anyone suffering from depression, addiction or substance abuse should seek medical help first and foremost. In my opinion, depression is your spirit urgently crying out for you to seek higher meaning. I believe this to be true for addiction as well. All forms of addiction are a spiritual hunger or thirst for deeper meaning.

- **Newfound self-knowledge**. Of course, finding out you are a sensitive person and your gentleness is a strength rather than a flaw is a giant spiritual awakening.

Be aware that spiritual awakening doesn't always have to be dramatic. Sometimes the need for change can creep up unawares, through everyday experiences, wonderful coincidences or during moments of bliss and calm or a connection to something greater than yourself. For example, it can be triggered by a stunning sunset, beautiful music, the kindness of a stranger, the unconditional love of a pet or anything that gives you feelings of awe and wonder.

If any of the above speak to you, then this is a powerful indicator that you are ready to live your life in a deeper and more meaningful way. Spiritual awakening does feel like a rebirth, and once you have begun your spiritual adventure, nothing in your life is ever the same again. You see that there is more to this life than meets the eye and you gain a much-needed sense of perspective. It's a thrilling experience. Sometimes the spiritual journey is depicted as serious and heavy, but it doesn't have to be that way. If you haven't done so already, do read James Redfield's classic, *The Celestine Prophecy*, which depicts spiritual growth as the exciting adventure it is.

Whatever triggers your search for deeper or higher meaning, the common factor will be that it turns the spotlight on your relationship with yourself. A sure-fire sign that you are awakening your spirituality is that you begin to understand, as never before, how essential self-love is for your personal growth and development.

Be cautious

Spiritual awakening is a captivating ride, and once it has begun you may be tempted to subscribe to or follow spiritual movements, philosophies, gurus and so on to guide you in the right direction. I have one piece of advice here: proceed with extreme caution.

Being a sensitive soul, you have likely spent your entire life trusting others readily. Sadly, the spiritual or New Age movement is unregulated and your trusting heart makes you susceptible to pseudo-spiritual babble and, for want of a better word, fraud. *The*

Sensitivity Code is designed to empower you to believe in yourself and your inner strength without relying on others to inform, fulfil or validate you. There are many so-called spiritual 'experts' out there, offering life coaching and personal growth and transformation advice in return for your attention, dependency and financial input.

A lot of spiritual 'advice' makes what should be natural and simple feel incredibly complex. You really don't need to meditate for hours or learn complicated rituals or words or attend hectic workshops. All you require is your loving heart and a belief in the eternal power of love to heal yourself and others.

There is nothing wrong with learning from others and opening your mind to perspectives and techniques offered by wise teachers, but if you find yourself becoming a follower of a guru, movement or programme, you become just that – a follower. You impose on your uniqueness the ideals and practices you are being taught. We all need role models to inspire us, but the problem is that each one of us is completely different, so however hard you try to follow or copy someone else, you won't succeed because you are not them. Your DNA is yours alone.

The universe will not see another person like you ever again, so why dilute what makes you original by trying to be someone you are not, however inspiring or spiritual that person may be? Be inspired by them by all means, but if you truly want to find your spiritual solution – and who you really are – perhaps the most important thing is to stop copying others.

However, emulating others isn't always wrong. When you are young and vulnerable and in need of firm guidance or support, copying may help you find your feet, but sooner or later, the individual spirit within you will demand recognition. There will come a time when you need to find out who you are and step into your own power. Walking your own spiritual path can be confusing and scary at first if you have become used to following or emulating others, but alongside the disorientation, you will also notice how alive you feel. It is intoxicating to finally become your authentic self, to truly be you.

Meeting yourself

The journey of self-discovery is lifelong, and along the way you will inevitably have moments of doubt and fear as well as moments of illumination. Whenever you are tempted to follow or copy others, think about what the world's greatest spiritual leaders have in common. Apart from their loving message of gentleness, they all share a secret, and that secret is very simple – these spiritual leaders did not follow or copy anyone else. Christ did not imitate and neither did Buddha or Muhammad. They found their own path – the one that worked for them. It is the same for you. Become an original. Don't lack confidence in yourself or just blindly follow the herd. Discover your own spiritual path. The best way to start doing that is to stop following and being like other people, and become who you are.

Whether you believe in an afterlife or not, read this wonderful parable daily as you begin to discover your authentic self.

> A great rabbi called Zusha lay crying on his deathbed. His students asked him why. After all, he had led an exemplary life filled with good deeds and he would surely be rewarded in heaven. Zusha told them he was crying because when he got to heaven, he knew God would not ask him, 'Why were you not more like Moses or King David?' God would ask him, 'Why were you not more like Zusha?' And he would not know what to say.

In other words, nobody can ever be absolutely as great as someone else, because no two people have exactly the same potential. But you can fulfil your own potential. Life is not a competition against anyone but yourself. Find the inner strength to be yourself.

You are enough.

As this book draws to a close, I hope it has inspired you to fall in love with yourself and your sensitive heart. I also hope it has helped you see that what makes you unique is your empathy, your intuition and your kindness and what makes you strong is your gentleness. There is an ocean of undiscovered potential in your sensitivity and you have the rest of your life to discover and fulfil that potential. You also have the rest of your life to learn that simply by being true to the love and kindness that is in your gentle heart, you are making a very real difference to the world.

To return to the possibility of an afterlife, I have often heard it said that the first spiritual being you meet in heaven isn't an angel or a departed loved one but the highest and best possible version of yourself. Unlocking the power of your sensitivity code can help you experience the bliss of meeting your best self in this life rather than the next. And then, when your time comes to close your eyes one last time, you will have lived the most fulfilling and deeply meaningful life of all – a heartfelt life, one which made a difference in the world because it was lived authentically and gently, without regrets.

Coming up...

The beginning of the rest of your life…

CONCLUSION

Kindred spirits

Once you remove all the false and negative perceptions about sensitivity that you have internalised, you can become the fiercely gentle person you were born to be. You can shine your light brightly. You can express your love, empathy, compassion, kindness and creativity without fear. Comfortable with who you are, you can become a force for great healing in the world. Simply by being true to yourself, and no longer hiding or pretending to be anything other than your gentle self, you can make your difference in the world.

Now is the perfect time to start applying in your daily life the tools and strategies this book has shared with you. They are powerful tools and will help set you on the right path and over time become the light to guide your way as you navigate the world.

I hope this book has also shown you that making a difference starts within you, within your own mind and heart. Confidence and meaning can't be bestowed on you by other people or things. It can't be found out there. It's already within you, and has been from the moment you took your first breath. You were born sensitive, and the world needs gentle people to show others what truly matters in life.

True grit

True strength is the opposite of what we have all been led to believe. It is not being forceful, loud, arrogant and powerful. It is being gentle to yourself and to others and understanding that sometimes gentleness requires you to set boundaries and calmly say no.

The strongest power in the world is gentleness, because gentleness does not provoke conflict or resistance or try to control or force. Gentle people hate hurting or upsetting others. Whereas conflict tears apart, gentleness unites, heals and inspires. It aims to understand, bring harmony and inspire peace. Gentleness is recognising similarities rather than differences. It is understanding that you can walk beside others without always agreeing. True grit is having the courage to be gentle, even if that means you must walk alone for a while. The world today urgently needs more sensitive people to discover within themselves the courage to show, rather than hide, their feelings. As you step into your own power, you will begin to understand that the purpose of your life is not to hide but to reveal your love, compassion and kindness. At first you may walk alone, but sooner or later you will attract into your life other sensitive souls who are also stepping into their own power. Like seeks like, remember. And when sensitive kindred spirits gather together, their collective power magnifies. They become the most powerful force in the world. The resources section will point you in the direction of online groups and communities of kindred spirits who celebrate the power and wonder of sensitive souls.

Born to be kind

People on their deathbeds don't talk about the money they have in the bank, how popular they are, how many likes and followers they have on social media, their incredible career, how much they are admired, their perfect teeth, spectacular holidays, luxury homes or fame. Rather, they talk about gentle moments of trust and kindness, and the deep feelings of love and connection that have uplifted and healed them. They talk about sensitive souls like *you* and the gentle gifts you reveal to the world or the sensitive times in their lives.

Please don't ever buy into the fake news that sensitivity is a weakness, feeling deeply is a flaw or that there is something wrong with you. This book has made it abundantly clear that there is absolutely *nothing* wrong with you. Your gentleness is your power. You were born to be kind because gentleness heals the world and makes this wonderful life feel beautiful. Never forget who you truly are: a bold, beautiful and stunningly sensitive soul.

'The tide recedes, but leaves behind bright seashells on the sand. The sun goes down, but gentle warmth still lingers on the land. The music stops, and yet it echoes on in sweet refrains... For every joy that passes, something beautiful remains.'

Martha Vashti Pearson

'In a gentle way, you can shake the world.'
Mahatma Gandhi

A LETTER FROM THERESA

Thank you from my heart for reading *The Sensitivity Code*. I felt both called and honored to write this book and truly hope that it has informed, guided and empowered you in some way.

If you did find the book helpful, and want to keep up to date with all my latest releases, just sign up at the following link. Your email address will never be shared and you can unsubscribe at any time.

www.thread-books.com/theresa-cheung

Details about how to get in touch with me if you have any questions to ask or stories to share can be found in the Resources, and if you enjoyed this book I would be deeply grateful if you could leave a review.

Getting feedback from readers is the reason I keep writing books. Your feedback also helps to persuade other readers to pick up one of my books, perhaps for the first time. Has this book inspired you? Has it helped? Have the tools and techniques spoken to you? Has *The Sensitivity Code* given you pause for thought and encouraged you to think about yourself and your life in a deeper way? If you are new to my writing, I hope you enjoy checking out my previous books and also stay tuned for my upcoming books with Bookouture.

Details about how to get in touch with me if you have any questions to ask or stories to share can be found in the Get in touch section, and if you enjoyed this book I would be deeply grateful if you could leave a review.

Thank you for letting my words accompany you a while on your incredible journey.

With love and gratitude,
Theresa xx

TheresaCheungAuthor

@theresa_cheung_author

@Theresa_Cheung

www.theresacheung.com

RESOURCES

Recommended reading

Aron, Elaine N, *The Highly Sensitive Child* (2002) Harmony Books

Aron, Elaine N, *The Highly Sensitive Parent* (2005) Citadel Press

Aron, Elaine N, *The Highly Sensitive Person* (1999) Thorsons

Aron, Elaine N, *The Highly Sensitive Person in Love* (2001) Harmony Books

Cain, Susan, *Quiet* (2013) Broadway Books

Cheung, Theresa, *The Premonition Code* (2018) Watkins Books

Cheung, Theresa, *21 Rituals to Ignite Your Intuition* (2019) Watkins Books

Cheung, Theresa, *The Dream Dictionary, A to Z* (2019) Thorsons

Chopra, Deepak, *The Seven Spiritual Laws of Success* (1994) New World Library

Hay, Louise, *You Can Heal Your Life* (1984) Hay House, Inc

Orloff, Judith, *The Empath's Survival Guide* (2017) Sounds True

Redfield, James, *The Celestine Prophecy* (1993) Grand Central Publishing

Tolle, Eckhart, *The Power of Now* (2016) Yellow Kite

TED talks about being sensitive

Karasinski, Laura, 'How to make your sensitivity your super-power', YouTube (uploaded 14 December 2016), https://www.youtube.com/watch?v=04bYPO5ORYE

Herdieckerhoff, Elena, 'The gentle power of highly sensitive people', YouTube (uploaded 24 June 2016), https://www.youtube.com/watch?v=pi4JOlMSWjo

Recommended websites/channels

www.hsperson.com

Dr Elaine Aron's website, which is a treasure trove of research and resources for sensitive souls.

www.drjudithorloff.com

Advice and support for empaths and intuitives.

www.hspinbusiness.com

Website for sensitive people to help advance their careers.

www.meetup.com

The place to search for highly sensitive person meetups.

www.highlysensitiverefuge.com

An online community to get inspiration and help turn your sensitivity into a powerful trait.

www.highlysensitive.org

Information for empaths and introverts.

www.melanietoniaevans.com

Advice and support for victims of narcissistic abuse.

https://www.youtube.com/channel/UC43mWclEzLjvVUT2jPs_7UA

Narc ology unscripted, a channel offering insight and support for empaths in toxic relationships.

https://youtu.be/EctzLTFrktc

Whatever you feel about Bezos this is a truly great speech about finding meaning and treasuring your gifts, whether you are sensitive or not.

www.noetic.org (IONS)

The science of consciousness and what connects us, plus research into meditation, energy healing and other spiritual practices that can heal and inspire.

www.noetic.org/Theresa-Cheung

Landing page gifted to me for my collaboration with the scientists researching consciousness at IONS. Three free gifts exclusively for Theresa Cheung readers available to download there.

www.theresacheung.com

Advice and support for sensitive souls offered via my email, *White Shores* podcast, social media channels and newsletter.

ACKNOWLEDGEMENTS

Deepest gratitude to my publisher, Claire Bord, for her vision and guidance and to Kim Nash for her kindness and support and for introducing me to Bookouture. Thanks also to Alexandra Holmes, Julie Fergusson, Peta Nightingale, Alex Crow, Rachel Rowlands and everyone at Bookouture involved in the production and promotion of this book. I'm also extremely thankful to Ingrid Court-Jones for her invaluable input while I researched and wrote this book.

The Sensitivity Code would not have felt complete without the voices of the extraordinary people who generously gave me permission to share their true-life stories and experiences here. I can't thank them enough, as they are truly authentic voices. I sincerely hope their contribution to this book will encourage other gentle souls to share their stories and spread the word about the power of gentleness to heal the world.

Sincere thanks to my wise agent Jane Graham Maw (www.grahammawchristie.com) for her patience and support. I am also forever in debt to all my wonderful readers, who are a never-ending source of inspiration to me. Last, but never least, heartfelt thanks to Ray, Robert and Ruthie (and my little dog, Arnie) for their love and support as I went into self-imposed exile to research and write this book.

ABOUT THE AUTHOR

Born into a family of sensitives and a highly sensitive person herself, *Sunday Times* bestselling author Theresa Cheung has a degree in Theology and English from the University of Cambridge. She has dedicated her writing career to championing the gentle traits of sensitive people and collating their stories. She has also been researching and writing about intuition, dreams, spirituality, holistic well-being and personal growth for the last 20 years.

Highly respected by scientists, psychologists and neurologists working in the same field, Theresa has built up a loyal readership and her numerous titles have been translated into dozens of languages. She has an impressive backlist that includes two *Sunday Times* top-10 bestsellers and many books that are consistently top of their categories on Amazon.

Theresa has had her work featured in national magazines and newspapers, including *Grazia*, *Prima*, the *Daily Mail*, the *Sunday Mirror*, the *Daily Express*, the *Sunday Observer* and the *Guardian*, most recently with her latest book *The Premonition Code*. She has been interviewed about being sensitive in an insensitive world by Russell Brand on episode 71 of his iconic podcast *Under the Skin* and by Piers Morgan on *Good Morning Britain*. She has also appeared on talkRADIO, various BBC radio stations, including BBC Radio 4 Beyond Belief, numerous spiritual and popular lifestyle podcasts, such as the award-winning *Lavendaire*, and has also launched her own podcast, *White Shores*.

Theresa's website is www.theresacheung.com.

GET IN TOUCH

The more that sensitive people share their stories and insights, the stronger and more visible we become. Please feel free to get in touch with me to share your own sensitivity stories and insights or to ask me questions. I'd love to hear from you. You can subscribe to my newsletter and contact me via my website, www.theresacheung.com. I can also be contacted via my Theresa Cheung Author Facebook, Instagram and Twitter pages or at my reader stories email address: angeltalk710@aol.com. Sometimes, if life gets a little overwhelming, it may take me a while to reply, but know that I intend to reply eventually to everyone who reaches out to me.

Made in the USA
Middletown, DE
22 May 2020